Sustainable Local Energy Planning and Decision Making:

Emerging Research and Opportunities

Vangelis Marinakis
National Technical University of Athens, Greece

A volume in the Practice, Progress, and Proficiency in Sustainability (PPPS) Book Series

www.igi-global.com

Published in the United States of America by
    IGI Global
    Information Science Reference (an imprint of IGI Global)
    701 E. Chocolate Avenue
    Hershey PA, USA 17033
    Tel: 717-533-8845
    Fax: 717-533-8661
    E-mail: cust@igi-global.com
    Web site: http://www.igi-global.com

Library of Congress Cataloging-in-Publication Data

Names: Marinakis, Vangelis, 1987- author.
Title: Sustainable local energy planning and decision making : emerging
  research and opportunities / by Vangelis Marinakis.
Description: Hershey, PA : Information Science Reference, 2017. | Includes
  bibliographical references.
Identifiers: LCCN 2016057759| ISBN 9781522522867 (hardcover) | ISBN
  9781522522874 (ebook)
Subjects: LCSH: Energy conservation--Planning. | Energy policy. | Energy
  consumption--Forecasting. | Sustainable development.
Classification: LCC TJ163.3 .M366 2017 | DDC 333.79/4--dc23 LC record available at https://lccn.
loc.gov/2016057759

This book is published in the IGI Global book series Practice, Progress, and Proficiency in
Sustainability (PPPS) (ISSN: 2330-3271; eISSN: 2330-328X)

British Cataloguing in Publication Data
A Cataloguing in Publication record for this book is available from the British Library.

All work contributed to this book is new, previously-unpublished material.
The views expressed in this book are those of the authors, but not necessarily of the publisher.

For electronic access to this publication, please contact: eresources@igi-global.com.

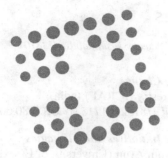

Practice, Progress, and Proficiency in Sustainability (PPPS) Book Series

ISSN:2330-3271
EISSN:2330-328X

Editor-in-Chief: Ayman Batisha, International Sustainability Institute, Egypt

MISSION

In a world where traditional business practices are reconsidered and economic activity is performed in a global context, new areas of economic developments are recognized as the key enablers of wealth and income production. This knowledge of information technologies provides infrastructures, systems, and services towards sustainable development.

The **Practices, Progress, and Proficiency in Sustainability (PPPS) Book Series** focuses on the local and global challenges, business opportunities, and societal needs surrounding international collaboration and sustainable development of technology. This series brings together academics, researchers, entrepreneurs, policy makers and government officers aiming to contribute to the progress and proficiency in sustainability.

COVERAGE

- Sustainable Development
- Green Technology
- Global Business
- Technological learning
- Strategic Management of IT
- Knowledge clusters
- Global Content and Knowledge Repositories
- Environmental Informatics
- ICT and knowledge for development
- Socio-Economic

IGI Global is currently accepting manuscripts for publication within this series. To submit a proposal for a volume in this series, please contact our Acquisition Editors at Acquisitions@igi-global.com or visit: http://www.igi-global.com/publish/.

Titles in this Series

For a list of additional titles in this series, please visit:
http://www.igi-global.com/book-series/practice-progress-proficiency-sustainability/73810

Sustainable Potato Production and the Impact of Climate Change
Sunil Londhe (International Centre for Research in Agroforestry (ICRAF),India)
Information Science Reference • ©2017 • 323pp • H/C (ISBN: 9781522517153) • US $180.00

Handbook of Research on Green Economic Development Initiatives and Strategies
M. Mustafa Erdoğdu (Marmara University, Turkey) Thankom Arun (University of Essex,
UK) and Imran Habib Ahmad (Global Green Growth Institute, SouthKorea)
Business Science Reference • ©2016 • 747pp • H/C (ISBN: 9781522504405) • US $335.00

Impact of Water Pollution on Human Health and Environmental Sustainability
A. Elaine McKeown (Independent Researcher, USA) and George Bugyi (Pennsylvania State
University, USA)
Information Science Reference • ©2016 • 422pp • H/C (ISBN: 9781466695597) • US $220.00

Impact of Meat Consumption on Health and Environmental Sustainability
Talia Raphaely (Curtin University, Australia) and Dora Marinova (Curtin University, Australia)
Information Science Reference • ©2016 • 410pp • H/C (ISBN: 9781466695535) • US $210.00

Handbook of Research on Pedagogical Innovations for Sustainable Development
Ken D. Thomas (Auburn University, USA) and Helen E. Muga (University of Mount Union,
USA)
Information Science Reference • ©2014 • 800pp • H/C (ISBN: 9781466658561) • US $345.00

Sustainability Science for Social, Economic, and Environmental Development
Nilanjan Ghosh (Multi Commodity Exchange of India Limited, India) and Anandajit Goswami
(The Energy and Resources Institute, India)
Information Science Reference • ©2014 • 324pp • H/C (ISBN: 9781466649958) • US $195.00

For an enitre list of titles in this series, please visit:
http://www.igi-global.com/book-series/practice-progress-proficiency-sustainability/73810

www.igi-global.com

701 East Chocolate Avenue, Hershey, PA 17033, USA
Tel: 717-533-8845 x100 • Fax: 717-533-8661
E-Mail: cust@igi-global.com • www.igi-global.com

Table of Contents

Preface

KEY ISSUES AND CHALLENGES

The current financial and economic crisis, as well as the wider socio-economic and environmental pressures, which include among others climate change, scarcity of natural resources, demographic change, social division and accelerated technological change, put seriously into question the traditional patterns of living, consuming and sharing resources (Koepper et al., 2009).

The European Commission launched the Europe 2020 Strategy to go out the crisis and prepare European Union (EU) economy as knowledge and innovation economy, capable of smart, sustainable and inclusive growth, with more and better jobs and greater social cohesion (EC, 2010). EU countries have also agreed on a new 2030 Framework for Climate and Energy, including EU-wide targets and policy objectives for the period between 2020 and 2030 (EC, 2014).

The European cities and communities have considerable importance, particularly with regard to new policies for local energy planning and sustainable development. They should be places of advanced social progress and environmental regeneration, as well as places of attraction and engines of economic growth, based on a holistic integrated approach, in which all aspects of sustainability are taken into account (EC, 2011). The disengagement from the unilateral economic development may be achieved through the progressive dissemination of renewable energy sources and energy efficiency. However, this inquires conditions' improvement, as regards financing, legal framework and administrative procedures. Europe will not be able to reach its commitments to alleviate climate change without the full participation and involvement of European municipalities (FREE, 2013).

The existence of high quality scientific workforce, high national and international interest for energy sustainability investments, a variety of existing financing sources, European initiatives towards the direct involvement of local authorities to the EU policy for climate change and the privileged geographic location comprise components of a mixture that can lead to sustainable development. In this context, several communities have proceeded to the adoption of a series of initiatives and actions by 2020 and beyond, taking into consideration that the local authorities' role is not limited to the provision of public services to citizens, but they ought to operate as a political, social and development body.

More specifically, the local governments demonstrate their willingness to implement sound local sustainable energy policies, especially through their participation in the Covenant of Mayors initiative (CoM, 2017a). The Covenant is the mainstream European movement involving local and regional authorities, voluntarily committing to increasing energy efficiency and use of renewable energy sources on their territories. The "Global Covenant of Mayors for Climate and Energy", a newly merged initiative between the Covenant of Mayors and the Compact of Mayors, aims at becoming the largest movement of local and regional authorities committed to going beyond their own national climate and energy objectives.

By their commitment, Covenant signatories aimed to meet and exceed the European Union 20% CO_2 reduction objective by 2020. New signatories now pledge to reduce CO_2 emissions by at least 40% by 2030 and to adopt an integrated approach to tackling mitigation and adaptation to climate change and so on (CoM, 2017b). The Sustainable Energy and Climate Action Plan is the key document in which the Covenant signatory outlines how it intends to reach its long-term CO_2 reduction target.

DECISION-MAKING PROBLEM

The Action Plans' elaboration and development constitutes a decision-making problem. The Decision Maker, namely the local authority (the Mayor and Municipal Council), in collaboration with the Analyst (Technical Manager) should identify all the actions and measures that will be integrated in the Sustainable Energy and Climate Action Plan of the municipality, taking into consideration the baseline energy and CO_2 emissions inventory. Active role in the planning process have interested stakeholders, such as energy agencies, investors, Energy Service Companies (ESCOs) and other companies offering energy related products, representatives of the local market and citizens (Marinakis et al., 2017).

However, many local and regional regions face particular challenges as regards growth, jobs and sustainability. These challenges include lower income levels, an unfavourable demographic situation, higher unemployment rates, a slower development of the tertiary sector, weaknesses in skills and human capital, a lack of opportunities for young people and a lack of necessary skills in parts of the agricultural sector and food processing industry (Marinakis et al., 2012; EU, 2012; EC, 2006). This situation has been aggravated by the financial and economic crisis in the current years.

In the international literature, existing studies propose methodologies and tools for the Action Plans' elaboration. There are methodologies that lay emphasis on the collection of energy data, while others provide alternative methods for stakeholders' engagement in the development of Action Plans. At the same time, some methodologies provide targeted guidance for different sectors of Action Plans, such as industry and transport. Moreover, relevant tools provide a series of guidelines.

However, the available methods and tools are not always well-adapted to local and regional communities. They do not offer an integrated framework for the development, implementation and monitoring of the Sustainable Energy and Climate Action Plans and especially the selection of the appropriate combination of renewable energy and energy efficiency actions and measures (Marinakis et al., 2017). As a result, there is the need for a decision support framework, appropriately customised to the local and regional communities' characteristics, addressing especially the interested stakeholders who are not "experts" in the field, saving resources and time. The methodology should be a useful instrument for local and regional authorities, facilitating sustainable local energy planning and decision making process.

Integrated Solutions for Sustainable Local Energy Planning

The main objective of this book is the presentation of an integrated methodological framework for the decision support of local and regional authorities towards sustainable energy planning. The scope is to contribute to the scientific "gap" regarding the development, implementation and monitoring of the Sustainable Energy and Climate Action Plan, aiming at the promotion of sustainable energy planning at the local - regional level. Based on the identification of the problem's parameters and their interrelations, the elaboration of a transparent and reliable decision support framework for the decision makers is achieved.

More specifically, this book contributes to the development of a coherent and transparent decision support framework for local energy planning, entitled "MPC+", consisted of the following four components:

- **"Map":** This component is the starting point of the Action Plan's development process. It includes the mapping of the current status within the region, giving particular emphasis on the energy and CO_2 emissions baseline. The results at this stage are the basis for the formulation of a comprehensive Action Plan.
- **"Plan":** This component focuses on the design of alternative Scenarios of Actions, namely a set of appropriate measures and actions for implementation at local - regional level. The design of scenarios is achieved through the modelling of measures and actions, the assessment of future trends in CO_2 emissions at local - regional level and the participation of local stakeholders.
- **"Choose":** This component aims to support decision makers in the process of identifying the most promising Scenario of Actions for the region. It includes the evaluation of the alternative Scenarios of Actions using multi-criteria analysis and robustness analysis.
- **"Check":** This component is related to the monitoring of the targets set in each activity sector of the city. In this way, the monitoring and assessment of the progress towards sustainable development in economic, social and environmental context is achieved.

In this context, standard techniques and tools have been developed and applied, such as multi-criteria ordinal regression approach, extreme ranking analysis, indicator-based assessment framework, participatory approach and aspiration levels, methods for the development of energy balance and estimation of the future emission trends at the local level.

Moreover, the "Action³" decision support system has been developed, incorporating the proposed "MPC+" framework, so as to guide the local and regional authorities, step-by-step, in the selection of the most appropriate combination of renewable energy and energy efficiency actions. A detailed description of the "BEI-Action", "MDS-Action" and "SEC-Action" modules for a successful implementation of local energy planning is provided. The proposed decision support system can be widely used by and support all types of cities and communities.

The pilot application of the proposed methodology (through the support of the information system developed) in real problem provided the possibility to evaluate its completeness and the results' reliability. An important element of the procedure for the assessment of the methodology was the direct communication with the local authorities and other stakeholders, as well as the availability of real data and reliable information within the framework of the European project "eReNet - Rural Web Energy Learning Network for Action" and particularly during the development of the Action Plan of the selected municipality.

From Energy Planning to Smart Energy Cities

In the process of building the future cities and communities, Information and Communication Technology (ICT) and Internet of Things (IoT) solutions are the key enablers. Cities are turning to advanced technologies to become Smart Cities. Smart Energy Cities, as a core pillar of the Smart Cities, constitute an emerging urban development strategy (Doukas et al., 2017).

Although there are plenty of energy related data available in the cities, there are no established methodologies and validated tools to collect, integrate and analyse them so that they can support energy use optimization (Androuaki et al., 2016). Intelligent and integrated assessment and consideration of various data sets, as well as relevant intelligent systems in a transparent and accessible manner is required.

In this context, the "Smart Cities IoT Platform" is introduced in this book. The "Smart Cities IoT Platform" integrates advanced ICT and IoT technologies in a single electronic web-based platform, in order to provide open, interoperable and holistic solutions for the city authorities and end-users of the residential, tertiary and industrial sector.

ORGANIZATION OF THE BOOK

This book contains five chapters, which are organized as follows:

Chapter 1: Decision Making in Local Energy Planning – A Review

This chapter describes the main issues of the decision making in local energy planning. The policy context and relevant initiatives are outlined. A detailed review of existing methodologies for local energy planning, as well as standard techniques and methods (participatory approach, aspiration level, multi-criteria decision support, robustness analysis, indicator-based assessment frameworks) are presented. The need to support the local and regional authorities in the decision making process for the development, implementation and monitoring of their Sustainable Energy and Climate Action Plans, especially within the framework of the Covenant of Mayors for Climate and Energy (a first-of-its-kind global initiative of cities and towns) is highlighted.

Chapter 2: Making Sustainable Energy Communities a Reality – The "MPC⁺" Decision Support Framework

The aim of this chapter is to present a decision support framework for local energy planning, entitled "MPC⁺ (Map - Plan - Choose - Check)". The proposed framework incorporates the development of the baseline emissions inventory, the identification and modelling of renewable energy and rational use of energy actions, as well as the creation of alternative Scenarios of Actions at the city level. The evaluation of alternative Scenarios is based on a multi-criteria ordinal regression approach. In addition, an extreme ranking analysis method is used, in order to examine robustness problems, estimating the best and worst possible ranking position of each Scenario. The MPC⁺ framework contributes to the selection of the most promising Scenario of renewable energy and rational use of energy actions, supporting the local and regional authorities in creating Sustainable Energy Communities. Finally, the "Methodological Approach for Monitoring SEC Targets" is introduced.

Chapter 3: An Intelligent Decision Support System for Sustainable Energy Local Planning

The main scope of this chapter is to present the "Action³" Decision Support System that integrates the MPC⁺ approach (Map - Plan - Choose - Check), supporting local and regional authorities to the development, implementation and monitoring of the Sustainable Energy and Climate Action Plan (especially within the framework of the Covenant of Mayors). The proposed intelligent system integrates three main modules, namely the "BEI-Action" for the development of the baseline emission inventory, the "MDS-Action" for the creation and evaluation of the alternative Scenarios of Actions aiming at the identification of the most promising Scenario, as well as the "SEC-Action" for the application of the "Methodological Approach for Monitoring SEC (Sustainable Energy Communities) Targets". The system was developed using the "Java" programming language and the "NetBeans IDE" software development platform. Particular emphasis was laid on the system's design, so as to be user-friendly, combining intuitive menus and navigation throughout the steps of the system.

Chapter 4: Developing and Monitoring a Sustainable Energy and Climate Action Plan for an Energy-Producing Community

The development, implementation and monitoring of the Sustainable Energy and Climate Action Plan require a significant amount of data and analysis, as well as an effective and comprehensive decision making process. This chapter presents the pilot application of the proposed "MPC+ (Map - Plan - Choose - Check)" framework, through the "Action[3]" Decision Support System, in a Greek energy-producing community. The pilot application is conducted in three phases, namely the development of the baseline emission inventory (Phase I), the creation and evaluation of alternative Scenarios of Actions (Phase II) and the monitoring of the actions and measures implemented (Phase III). The city's univocal economy orientation of energy production through lignite is considered as a basic, inhibitory factor towards sustainability. In this respect, the city has committed to implement a series of appropriate renewable energy and rational use of energy activities in its territory, laying balanced emphasis on the local energy and heat production, and the promotion and implementation of measures on energy savings. A significant part of the CO_2 emissions' reduction will come from the installation of biomass district heating systems in local communities.

Chapter 5: Building Future "Smart Energy Cities" – The Role of ICT and IoT Solutions

The aim of this chapter is to present the "Smart Cities IoT Platform". A "wireless telemetry cloud" over the city can be created, which facilitates the transferring of open data from the distributed sources (weather station, installed equipment, etc.). The proposed IoT Platform is composed of prediction models, scenarios and rules, as well as a database to store the data and results. With the Smart Cities IoT Platform, web-based applications can be created, customised to the specific characteristics and needs of end-users, including the fields of buildings, infrastructure, transport, generation and storage.

CONCLUSION

The contribution towards addressing the climate change problem, through the communities' CO_2 emissions reduction and the creation of sustainable jobs, strengthening the extraverted economic activity at local level, can comprise the success measure of this particular effort. One of the bets to be won includes the liberation of local authorities from their role to promote infrastructure projects without central planning and their connection with sustainable development's strategic goals. The European cities have to work towards the direction of strengthening the areas' benefits, by taking advantage of existing opportunities at national and European level, in order to achieve sustainable development.

REFERENCES

Androulaki, S., Doukas, H., Marinakis, V., Madrazo, L., & Legaki, N. Z. (2016). Enabling Local Authorities to Produce Short-Term Energy Plans: A Multidisciplinary Decision Support Approach. *Management of Environmental Quality*, *27*(2), 146–166. doi:10.1108/MEQ-02-2014-0021

CoM - Covenant of Mayors. (2017a). *Covenant in Figures*. Retrieved January 21, 2017, from: http://www.covenantofmayors.eu/about/covenant-in-figures_en.html

CoM - Covenant of Mayors. (2017b). *The Covenant of Mayors for Climate and Energy Reporting Guidelines*. Covenant of Mayors Office & Joint Research Centre of the European Commission. Retrieved January 21, 2017, from: http://www.covenantofmayors.eu/IMG/pdf/Covenant_ReportingGuidelines.pdf

Doukas, H., Marinakis, V., Spiliotis, V., & Psarras, J. (2017). *OPTIMUS Decision Support Tools: Transforming Multidisciplinary Data to Energy Management Action Plans*. IEEE – 7th International Conference on Information, Intelligence, Systems and Applications (IISA 2016).

EC - European Commission. (2006). Communication from the Commission to the Council and the European Parliament: Employment in Rural Areas: Closing the Jobs Gap. COM(2006) 857 final. Brussels, Belgium: EC.

EC - European Commission. (2010). *Communication from the Commission Europe 2020 - A strategy for Smart, Sustainable and Inclusive Growth*. COM(2010) 2020 final.

EC - European Commission. (2011). Cities of Tomorrow – Challenges, visions, ways forward. Brussels, Belgium: EC.

EC - European Commission. (2014). *2030 Climate and Energy Framework*. Retrieved February 11, 2017, from: https://ec.europa.eu/clima/policies/strategies/2030_en

EU - European Union. (2012). *Rural Development in the EU Statistical and Economic: Information Report 2012*. Brussels, Belgium: Directorate-General for Agriculture and Rural Development.

FREE - Future of rural Energy in Europe. (2013). *Rural Myths and Realities*. Retrieved September 18, 2016, from: http://www.rural-energy.eu

Koepper, J., Pavese, N., Gonzalez, I. A., & Birnstill, M. (2009). *A CSR Europe Helpdesk Service: Integration of CSR/Sustainable Development into Performance Assessments and Evaluation Processes at Large Companies*. Brussels, Belgium: CSR Europe.

Marinakis, V., Doukas, H., Xidonas, P., & Zopounidis, C. (2017). Multicriteria Decision Support in Local Energy Planning: An Evaluation of Alternative Scenarios for the Sustainable Energy Action Plan. *Omega – The International Journal of Management Science*.

Marinakis, V., Papadopoulou, A., & Psarras, J. (2012). Strengthening Sustainable Energy Policies within the Covenant of Mayors Initiative. *Proceedings of the 5th International Scientific Conference on "Energy and Climate Change"*.

Marinakis, V., Papadopoulou, A., & Psarras, J. (2017). Local Communities towards a Sustainable Energy Future: Needs and Priorities. *International Journal of Sustainable Energy*, *36*(3), 296–312. doi:10.1080/14786451.2015.1018264

Chapter 1
Decision Making in Local Energy Planning:
A Review

ABSTRACT

The current financial and economic crisis, as well as the wider socioeconomic and environmental pressures, including climate change among others, put seriously into question the traditional development patterns. This is particularly true for the local and regional authorities, who face a number of challenges as regards growth, jobs and sustainability. These pressures create high expectations for coordinated actions and holistic interventions to address comprehensively the problems toward a competitive economy. In this context, this Chapter describes the main issues of the decision making in local energy planning. The policy context and relevant initiatives are outlined. A detailed review of existing methodologies for local energy planning, as well as standard techniques and methods (participatory approach, aspiration level, multi-criteria decision support, robustness analysis, indicator-based assessment frameworks) are presented. The need to support the local and regional authorities in the decision-making process for the development, implementation and monitoring of their Sustainable Energy and Climate Action Plans, especially within the framework of the Covenant of Mayors for Climate and Energy (a first-of-its-kind global initiative of cities and towns) is highlighted.

DOI: 10.4018/978-1-5225-2286-7.ch001

INTRODUCTION

The current financial and economic crisis, as well as the wider socioeconomic and environmental pressures, which include climate change, scarcity of natural resources, demographic change, social division, accelerated technological change, and many more, put seriously into question the traditional patterns of living, consuming, and sharing resources (Koepper et al., 2009). These pressures create high expectations for coordinated actions and holistic interventions to address comprehensively the problems of modern society and competitive economy. In particular, with regard to energy and environment issues, integrated approaches and methodological frameworks are the key challenge for policy and decision-makers in order to embark them on strategies toward sustainable development and scientifically optimize energy concepts for the future (Doukas et al., 2012a; Deilmann and Bathe 2009; Stigson et al., 2009).

The importance of taking immediately action to prevent and address climate change and its environmental impacts is explicitly recognized both on political and on social level (Omer, 2008). A number of studies, such as the Stern Review on the economics of climate change (Stern 2007) reaffirms the enormous costs of inaction, as well as other relevant researches (Oxfam International 2007; UNDP 2007; UNFCCC 2007; World Bank 2009; Lund, 2007) note that developing countries will need more than 50 billion US dollars per year to tackle climate change, and far more if global emissions are not cut rapidly. In addition, the communication of the European Union (EU) in 2005, "Winning the battle against global climate change," indicated that the benefits of limiting climate change outweigh the costs of taking action (EC, 2005). Thus, mitigation of climate change and its environmental impacts is technically feasible and affordable, provided that not only an integrated and comprehensive approach in community and national policy level be followed, but also the emissions producers act immediately.

The EU had always put high in its agenda activities related to the attainment of economic growth and prosperity. The EU 2020 sustainable development vision provides an opportunity to support the global fight against climate change (EC, 2011a). The EU Climate and Energy Package (EC, 2008) has set very ambitious targets for sustainable development, known as the "20-20-20" targets for 2020 (Figure 1).

Figure 1. "20-20-20" targets for 2020

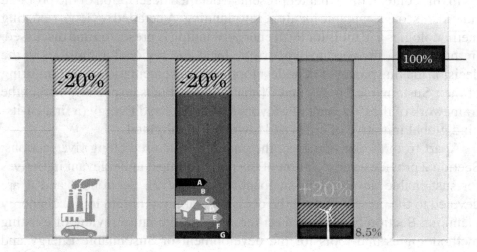

In the context of Europe 2020 strategy, a comprehensive strategic approach has been put forward for the next decade to foster inclusive and sustainable growth in Europe and to provide a framework for the EU to emerge strengthened from the current financial and economic crisis (EC, 2010c). Moreover, EU countries have agreed on a new 2030 Framework for climate and energy, including EU-wide targets and policy objectives for the period between 2020 and 2030 (EC, 2014):

- A 40% cut in greenhouse gas emissions compared to 1990 levels.
- At least a 27% share of renewable energy consumption.
- At least 27% energy savings compared with the business-as-usual scenario.

The Europe 2020 Strategy has been implemented in partnership with Europe's regions and communities, as the key actors who can close the "delivery" gap (EU, 2013).

National prosperity is created, not inherited. The European municipalities have considerable importance, particularly with regard to new policies for local energy planning and sustainable development (Porter, 1990).

In this context, this Chapter presents a detailed description of the problem statements for sustainable local energy planning. A detailed review of existing methodologies and tools for local energy planning is presented and discussed. In this respect, the need to support the local and regional authorities in the decision making process for the development, implementation and monitoring of their Sustainable Energy and Climate Action Plans, especially within the framework of the Covenant of Mayors for Climate and Energy (a first-of-its-kind global initiative of cities and towns) is highlighted.

Apart from the introduction, the paper is structured along five sections. Section 2 provides a description of the policy context and relevant initiatives for sustainable development at local/regional level. Sections 3 and 4 are devoted to the presentation of the decision making problem for local energy planning. Section 5 is devoted on the relevant literature review of existing methodologies and tools for the development of Sustainable Energy and Climate Action Plans. Finally, the last section just summarizes the key issues that have arisen in this Chapter.

POLICY CONTEXT AND RELEVANT INITIATIVES

The European cities should be places of advanced social progress and environmental regeneration, as well as places of attraction and engines of economic growth based on a holistic integrated approach in which all aspects of sustainability are taken into account (EC, 2011c). A number of European initiatives have been launched related to these ideas, as presented in the following paragraphs.

The municipalities, as consumers, demonstrate their willingness to implement sound local sustainable energy policies, especially through their participation in the Covenant of Mayors initiative[1]. The Covenant is the mainstream European movement involving local and regional authorities, voluntarily committing to increasing energy efficiency and use of renewable energy sources on their territories. The new "Global Covenant of Mayors for Climate and Energy", a newly merged initiative between the Covenant of Mayors and the Compact of Mayors, aims at becoming the largest movement of local governments committed to going beyond their own national climate and energy objectives. By their commitment, Covenant signatories aimed to meet and exceed the European Union 20% CO_2 reduction objective by 2020. New signatories now pledge to reduce CO_2 emissions by at least 40% by 2030 and to adopt an integrated approach to tackling mitigation and adaptation to climate change (CoM, 2017a).

The Energy-efficient Buildings Public Private Partnership in research (EC, 2010b), launched under the European Economic Recovery Plan, represents the initial and highly strategic step of a longer term set by the industry to create more efficient districts and cities while improving the quality of life of European citizens. This initiative aims to address the challenges that the European construction sector and its extended value chain are facing in their ambitious goal of researching new methods and technologies to reduce the energy footprint and CO_2 emissions related to new and renovated buildings. Specific attention will be given to the development and integration of design and simulation tools, new materials, building systems and equipment and ICT for energy efficiency. In addition, the Directive 2010/31/EU (EPBD recast) has pointed out the leading role of the public sector in the field of energy performance of buildings, as new buildings occupied and owned by public authorities should be nearly zero-energy buildings, after 31 December 2018.

The European Innovation Partnership (EIP) on Smart Cities and Communities (SCC) was launched in July 2012 to achieve a meaningful large-scale deployment of smart city solutions in Europe, focusing on the intersections of ICT, energy and transport (EC, 2012). The European municipalities themselves have also taken a very pro-active role and launched the Green Digital Charter in 2009. The municipalities signing up to the Charter commit to reduce the carbon footprint of their ICT and roll-out ICT solutions which lead to more energy efficiency in areas such as buildings, transport and energy. The SCC partnership bridges the areas of energy and ICT with the objective to catalyse progress in the areas of energy production, distribution and use; and ICT are intimately linked and offer new interdisciplinary opportunities to improve services while reducing energy and resource consumption and Greenhouse Gas (GHG) and other polluting emissions. The SCC will go beyond coordinating research and innovation projects and will tackle demand side measures such as enhancing new business models for energy and ICT services.

The Smart Cities Stakeholder Platform is essentially about promoting innovation. It aims to accelerate the development and market deployment of energy efficiency and low-carbon technology applications in the urban environment. The Platform supports the EU towards its goal of an 80% reduction of GHG emissions by 2050 and the Europe's primary energy technology policy, the SET-Plan.

The European Energy Research Alliance (EERA) Joint Programme on Smart Cities was launched in September 2010. Its main objective is the development of scientific tools and methods that will enable an intelligent design, planning and operation of the energy system of an entire city in the near future. An integrated approach will be adopted for the planned research activities in order to capture the interfaces between all the relevant elements of the energy system, such as thermal and electric energy networks, buildings, energy supply technologies and the end-user.

Finally, two of the flagships of Europe 2020 strategy are the Digital Agenda for Europe and the resource-efficient Europe:

- **Digital Agenda for Europe (EC, 2010a):** The Digital Agenda for Europe provides a policy framework aiming at delivering sustainable economic and social benefits from a digital single market based on fast and ultra-fast internet and interoperable applications. In this context, the EU promotes the effective use of ICTs to address societal challenges in energy, climate, and resource efficiency. This includes initiatives in areas such as sustainable cities, energy efficient buildings, smart energy grids and climate change management. Cooperation between the public authorities and ICT sector is essential to accelerate development and wide-scale roll out of ICT-based solutions for smart grids and meters and near-zero energy buildings. The ICT sector should deliver modelling, analysis, monitoring and visualisation tools to evaluate the energy performance and emissions of buildings, cities and regions. For the different grids to work together efficiently and safely, open transmission-distribution interfaces will be needed.
- **Resource-Efficient Europe (EC, 2011b):** The flagship initiative for a resource-efficient Europe under the Europe 2020 strategy supports the shift towards a resource-efficient, low-carbon economy to achieve sustainable growth. To enjoy the benefits of a resource-efficient and low-carbon economy, three conditions need to be fulfilled:
  ◦ First, coordinated action in a wide range of policy areas, action in need of political visibility and support;
  ◦ Secondly, urgent action due to long investment lead-times. While some actions will have a positive impact on growth and jobs in the short-term, others require an upfront investment and have long pay-back times, but will bring real economic benefits for the EU economy for decades to come;

○   Thirdly, necessary is the empowerment of consumers in order to move to resource-efficient consumption, to drive continuous innovation and ensure that efficiency gains are not lost.

DECISION MAKING PROBLEM FOR LOCAL ENERGY PLANNING

Europe will not be able to reach its commitments to alleviate climate change without the full participation and involvement of the European municipalities. Not only does the local population need to be able to make the right energy choices, but most of the renewable and energy efficiency options, from wind farms, to solar, to combined heat and power, will require the willing participation of communities (FREE, 2013).

At the 6th European Summit of Regions and Cities in Athens (7-8 March 2014) the Bureau of the Committee of the Regions adopted a declaration on the mid-term review of Europe 2020, titled "A Territorial Vision for Growth and Jobs" (CoR, 2014a). The political declaration argues that the future success of the EU's growth strategy hinges on better engagement of local and regional authorities. In addition, a handbook has been developed as a part of the follow up to the adopted Committee's opinion on the role of local and regional authorities in achieving the objectives of the Europe 2020 strategy (CoR, 2014b).

As mentioned above, the Covenant of Mayors for Climate and Energy constitutes a first-of-its-kind global initiative of cities and towns committed transparent climate action. The Sustainable Energy and Climate Action Plan is the key document in which the Covenant signatory outlines how it intends to reach its long-term CO_2 reduction target. The target sectors are the buildings, equipment, facilities and transport. The sustainable energy policy may also include actions related to the local electricity production (development of photovoltaics, wind power, combined heat and power, improvement of local power generation) and local heating/cooling generation (EC, 2010d). Nowadays, the Covenant of Mayors initiative counts more than 7,200 signatories. In addition, more than 5,600 Action Plans have been submitted (CoM, 2017b).

According to Marinakis et al. (2017a), Action Plans' elaboration and development is a decision making problem (Figure 2). The decision maker, namely the local authority (the Mayor and Municipal Council), in collaboration

Figure 2. Decision-making process for the elaboration and development of sustainable energy and climate action plans

with the Analyst (Technical Manager) should identify all the actions and measures that will be integrated in the Action Plan of the local community, taking into consideration the baseline energy and CO_2 emissions inventory. They should also identify the overall goal of CO_2 emissions reduction by 2030 (at least 40%).

Active role in the planning process have interested stakeholders, such as energy centres, investors, companies, representatives of the local market and citizens. According to Renn et al (1993), stakeholders, experts and citizens should each contribute to the planning effort, through their particular expertise and experience. The benefits of combining participatory methods with analytical tools are widely acknowledged (Kowalski et al., 2009; Madlener et al., 2007).

Despite the high number of signatories, the lack of proper information and communication about the Covenant of Mayor's initiative and the obligations arising from its signing seems to be preventing the realization of the initiative's full potential (Christoforidis et al., 2013; 2011). In local and regional environments, fulfilling the Covenant's commitment of submitting a Sustainable Energy and Climate Action Plan within a one-year timeframe can come with very challenging constraints. Some communities, and in particular those which are most remote, depopulated or dependent on agriculture, already face particular challenges as regards growth, jobs and sustainability

(Marinakis et al., 2012a, 2012b; Doukas et al., 2012b). These challenges include lower income levels, an unfavourable demographic situation, higher unemployment rates, a slower development of the tertiary sector, weaknesses in skills and human capital, a lack of opportunities for young people and a lack of necessary skills in parts of the agricultural sector and food processing industry (Marinakis et al., 2012c; EU, 2012; EC, 2006). This situation has been aggravated by the financial and economic crisis in the current years.

REVIEW OF EXISTING METHODOLOGIES AND TOOLS

Tools and Methods for Action Plans' Development

In the international literature, many existing studies propose methodologies and tools for the Action Plans' development and elaboration from relevant activities and mainly Intelligent Energy Europe (IEE) co-financed projects (Marinakis et al., 2017b). A first study was presented by Bertoldi et al. (2009). Figure 3 presents an overview of all the available methodologies and tools that have been developed so far (CLIMATE COMPASS, 2006; COMBAT, 2008; CoM, 2013; ENNEREG, 2013; Covenant CapaCITY, 2013; ENOVA, 2012; ENSRC, 2011; MAKE-IT-BE, 2011; Moving Sustainably Project, 2011; TMCE, 2011; 100-RES-COMMUNITIES, 2010; Energie-Cites, 2008; MODEL, 2008; PEPESEC, 2008; SEC-Tools, 2008; SECURE, 2008; European Energy Award, 2007; ICLEI, 2007; MUSEC, 2007; Wise Plans, 2007; Minnesota Project et al., 2003).

There are methodologies that lay emphasis on the collection of energy data, while others provide alternative methods for stakeholders' engagement in the development of Action Plans. At the same time, some methodologies provide targeted guidance for different sectors of Action Plans, such as industry and transport. Moreover, relevant tools provide a series of guidelines, such as "Toolbox of Methodologies on Climate & Energy" (TMCE, 2013)", "Covenant capaCITY Training Platform (Covenant CapaCITY, 2013)" and "CoMO's e-learning (CoM, 2013)".

However, available methods and tools are not always well-adapted to cities and local/regional communities (Marinakis et al., 2017b, 2015). Moreover, they do not offer an integrated framework for the development of Sustainable Energy and Climate Action Plans and especially the selection of the appropriate combination of renewable energy and rational use of energy technologies.

Figure 3. Tools and methods for the development of sustainable energy and climate action plans (Marinakis et al., 2017b)

	Stakeholders' Participation	Decision Support System	Technoeconomic Evaluation	Monitoring & Evaluation	Building, Equipment & Facilities	Industry	Transport	Local Energy Production	Agriculture Sector
BELIEF	★	★★★	★	★	☐	☐	☑	☐	☑
Climate Compass	★★★	★	★	★★★	☐	☐	☑	☑	☐
COMBAT Report guidelines	★★	★★★	★	★★	☑	☑	☑	☑	☐
CoMO's e-learning	★★	★★	★★	★★	☑	☑	☑	☑	☐
Covenant capaCITY	★★	★★	★	★★	☑	☐	☑	☐	☐
ENNEREG	★	★★★	★	★	☑	☑	☑	☑	☐
ENOVA	★★	★	★	★	☑	☑	☑	☑	☐
ENSRC	★	★★	★	★	☑	☐	☑	☑	☑
European Energy Award	★★	★★	★★	★★	☑	☑	☑	☑	☐
ICLEI / Natural Capitalism	★★	★★★	★	★★	☑	☑	☑	☑	☐
Make it Be	★	★★	★	★★	☑	☑	☑	☑	☐
Minnesota Project	★	★★★	★	★	☐	☐	☐	☑	☐
MODEL	★★★	★	★★★	★★	☐	☐	☐	☐	☐
Moving Sustainably	★★	★★★	★★	★★	☐	☐	☑	☐	☐
MUSEC	★★	★★	★	★★	☑	☑	☑	☑	☐
PEPESEC	★★	★★	★	★	☑	☑	☑	☐	☐
SEC Tools	★★★	★	★★★	★	☑	☐	☑	☑	☐
Secure Project	★★	★★★	★	★	☑	☐	☑	☑	☐
Toolbox of Methodologies	★★★	★★	★	★★	☑	☑	☑	☑	☐
Wise Plans	★★	★★★	★★	★	☑	☑	☑	☑	☐
100-RES-COMMUNITIES	★	★★	★★★	★★	☐	☐	☐	☐	☑

Participatory Approach

All members of the society have a key role in establishing a common vision for the future and defining the paths that will make this vision come true. Indeed, their views should be integrated in the alternative Scenarios for the region. In this respect, the participatory approach can stimulate the behavioural changes that are needed to complement the Action Plans' measures.

The benefits of combining participatory methods with analytical tools are widely acknowledged (Kowalski et al., 2009; Stagl, 2007; Munda, 2004; Polatidis & Haralambopoulos, 2004; Geurts & Joldersma, 2001). Different ways to consider participatory approach have been identified, such as "Information", "Consultation", "Deciding together", "Acting together" and "Supporting independent community initiatives" (CTB, 2014). In any case, the participation in planning could improve the quality, acceptance and effectiveness of the alternative action plans for the region.

Aspiration Level

The local authorities set the minimum longer-term target in percentage of CO_2 emissions reduction. According to the Covenant's guidelines, the target should be a minimum of 20% reduction by 2020 or 40% reduction by 2030. However, the local authorities can define a different longer-term target. This means that the examined actions and measures for the region should achieve this longer-term target. To this end, an aspiration level regarding CO_2 emissions reduction of each alternative is used, working as a filtering for the identification of feasible Scenarios.

A number of studies exist on the aspiration level approach (Nowak, 2007). More specifically, Wang and Zionts (2006) examined the relationship between aspiration levels and their mapped-to solutions in the MCDA context. Yun et al. (2004) presented an aspiration level approach using generalized data envelopment analysis and genetic algorithms in multiple criteria decision making such as engineering design problems. In the study of Granat and Makowski (2000), the specified aspiration levels are used for the generation of component achievement functions for corresponding criteria, which reflect the degree of satisfaction of results.

Multicriteria Decision Support

Multiple Criteria Decision Aid (MCDA) methods can be an important supportive tool in policy making, providing the potential to evaluate the alternatives' implications to the environmental, economical and social axes (Doukas et al., 2010; Wang et al., 2009). In decision-making involving multiple criteria, the basic problem stated by analysts and decision-makers concerns the way that the final decision should be made (Doukas et al., 2007). The main idea of the available MCDA methods, is to create a more standardized and structured process for decision making (Doukas et al., 2014; Greening and Bernow, 2004).

In the international literature, there are studies that present applications of Multicriteria Analysis on specific issues related to sustainable energy planning (Table 1). However, none of these studies offer an integrated framework for the Action Plans' development and especially the selection of the most appropriate sustainable renewable energy and rational use of energy technologies at local - regional level.

11

Table 1. MCDA in energy and environmental issues

Method	Authors	Application Area
Analytic Hierarchy Process (AHP)	Balo & Şağbanşua (2016)	photovoltaic System Design
	Sindhu et al. (2016)	recognition and prioritization of challenges in growth of solar energy
	Domenech et al. (2015)	electrification systems for rural communities
	Lanjewar et al. (2015)	assessment of alternative fuels for transportation
	Erol & Kilkis (2012)	energy source policy assessment
	Meyar & Vaez (2012)	energy policy making
	Awasthi & Chauhan (2011)	sustainable transport solutions
	Shen et al. (2011)	renewable energy sources
	Tegou et al. (2010)	environmental management
ELECTRE	Mousavi et al. (2017)	renewable energy policy
	Jun et al. (2014)	selection of wind/solar hybrid power station
	Rojas-Zerpa & Yusta (2014)	electric supply planning in rural remote areas
	Catalina et al. (2011)	multi-source energy systems
	Haurant et al. (2011)	photovoltaic plants
	Özkan et al. (2011)	solid waste management system
	Papadopoulos et. (2008)	decentralised energy systems
	Beccali et al. (2003)	decision-making in energy planning
Multi-Attribute Utility Theory (MAUT)	Volvačiovas et al., (2013)	public buildings retrofits strategy
	Kalbar et al. (2012)	wastewater treatment technology
	Kambezidis et al. (2011)	renewable energy sources
	Voropai & Ivanova (2002)	electric power system
	Pan et al. (2000)	strategic resource planning
PROMETHEE	Kuang et al. (2015)	evaluation of source water protection strategies
	Ghafghazi et al. (2010)	district heating system
	Cavallaro (2009)	concentrated solar thermal technologies
	Terrados et al. (2009)	renewable energy planning
	Tsoutsos et al. (2009)	sustainable energy planning
TOPSIS	Aalami et al. (2010)	demand response programs
	Boran et al. (2012)	electricity generation
	Lee & Lin (2011)	energy performance of buildings
UTA	Marinakis et al. (2017)	local energy planning
	Sola & Mota (2012)	industrial motor systems
	Demesouka et al. (2013)	wastewater treatment
	Kholghi (2001)	wastewater planning management

In the traditional aggregation paradigm, the criterion aggregation model is known a priori, while the global preference is unknown. On the contrary, the philosophy of disaggregation involves the inference of preference models from given global preferences (Siskos, 2001). The philosophy of preference disaggregation in multicriteria analysis is to assess/infer preference models from given preferential structures and to address decision-aiding activities through operational models. The existence of the preference model assumes the preferential independence of the criteria for the decision maker (Keeney and Raiffa, 1976), while other conditions for additivity have been proposed by Fishburn (1966, 1967). This assumption does not pose significant problems in a posteriori analyses, such as disaggregation analyses.

Robustness Analysis

The evaluation models of the multicriteria analysis are generally based on a set of acceptances, assumptions and estimations. These elements are often characterized by a high degree of uncertainty, given the complexity and uncertainty of the decision making environment (Hites et al., 2006). In this respect, another important issue is the robustness of the evaluation model (Roy, 2010). This fact has caused the intense interest of the research community. The recent studies focus on the development of integrated procedures for the robustness's analysis and measurement in different multicriteria analysis methods, as well as how these methods can adapt existing techniques to achieve the formation of stable solutions (Mavrotas et al., 2015; Siskos & Tsotsolas, 2015; Fliege & Werner, 2014). Some of the most recent UTA-type methods are UTA^{GMS}, GRIP, RUTA, extreme ranking analysis and robustness measurement control (Greco et al., 2008; Figueira et al., 2009; Kadzinski et al., 2013; Kadzinski et al. (2012); Kadzinski & Tervonen, 2013a, 2013b; Greco et al., 2012).

Indicator-Based Assessment Frameworks

In May 2014, the Covenant of the Mayors published a special guide for the monitoring of Action Plans. In this context, the "Implementation Report" should include quantitative data regarding the measures implemented, their impact on the energy consumption and the CO_2 emission. Additionally, an analysis of the actions' implementation should be enclosed, including the required corrective measures. Consequently, use of indicators is necessary for evaluating the progress of the Sustainable Energy and Climate Action Plan.

The indicators are a decision making methodological tool, as they quantify and simplify phenomena, in order to provide a better understanding of a complex reality. They represent mainly quantitative information and they elaborate different and multiple data (Androulaki et al., 2016). Different research teams have examined the basic parameters for the selection of the indicators (Rees et al. 2008, Niemeijer & de Groot, 2008). The selection of the indicators strongly depends on the nature and the goal of the researchers and the decision makers. During the selection of the indicators, criteria concerning the completeness, the adaptability and the appropriateness must be taken into account.

The literature review for the development of energy related indicators shows that the most important attempts, are located in big international organizations, focused on the following fields: environment, sustainable development, energy use and energy efficiency. "OECD (Organization for Economic Development and Cooperation)" operates in the field of environmental information; it has managed to develop a collection of directly related indicators and many collections of indexes for various fields (e.g. indicators for energy-environment, indicators for transportation-environment, etc.) The indicators for energy-environment have been developed to promote and to strengthen the integration of environmental worries in the development of the OECD countries' energy policy.

In practice, the scientific community uses composite indexes. Namely, the value of a composite index is a function of two or more individual indicators which are related to a system or a phenomenon (OECD, 2002). The proper description of such an index requires a careful selection of the individual indicators and their weighting factors. One of the main composite indexes commonly used is the Environmental Performance Index (EPI, 2015). It is a method of quantitative and numerical comparative evaluation of the environmental performances of a country and its policies.

The development of composite indexes in the field of sustainable energy planning is limited in the international literature (Evans et al., 2009; Vera & Langlois, 2007; Afgan et al., 2000). Brown & Sovacool (2007) suggested an energy sustainability index to evaluate energy policy. Abouelnaga et al. (2010) have studied the sustainable nuclear energy indicator, while Afgan et al. (2005) focused on the modelling of sustainable development indicator.

CONCLUSION

Nowadays, sustainable energy policy has been a challenge for the local authorities. The contribution towards addressing the climate change problem, through the communities' CO_2 emissions' reduction and the creation of sustainable jobs, strengthening the extraverted economic activity at local and regional level, can comprise the success measure of this particular effort. One of the bets to be won includes the liberation of local authorities from their role to promote infrastructure projects without central planning and their connection with sustainable development's strategic goals. The disengagement from the unilateral economic development may be achieved through the progressive dissemination of renewable energy and rational use of energy actions.

The European cities have to work towards the direction of strengthening the areas' benefits, by taking advantage of existing opportunities at national and European level, in order to achieve sustainable development. As a result, the decision making problem of Action Plans' elaboration and development within the framework of Covenant's initiative is an important component in local authorities' operation towards the creation of sustainable energy communities.

The cities and communities possess a significant potential for renewable energy and rational use of energy projects implementation in order to proceed towards energy sustainability. Although the local authorities demonstrate their willingness to implement sound local sustainable energy policies, especially through their participation in the Covenant of Mayors' initiative, it seems that this underlying potential remains largely unexploited. Indeed, the lack of technical capacity and the limited resources are the most important barriers for the local and regional authorities.

However, available methods and tools are not always well-adapted to cities and local/regional communities. They do not offer an integrated framework for the development, implementation and monitoring of the Sustainable Energy and Climate Action Plans and especially the selection of the appropriate combination of renewable energy and energy efficiency actions and measures. As a result, there is the need for a methodological framework, appropriately customised to the local and regional communities' characteristics, addressing especially the interested stakeholders who are not "experts" in the field, saving resources and time. The methodology should be a useful instrument for local and regional authorities, facilitating sustainable local energy planning and decision making process.

ACKNOWLEDGMENT

A part of the current chapter was based on the relevant activities conducted within the framework of the project "Rural Web Energy Learning Network for Action – eReNet (Project no: IEE/10/224/SI2.593412), supported by the Intelligent Energy – Europe (IEE) Programme. The content of the Chapter is the sole responsibility of its author and does not necessary reflect the views of the EC.

REFERENCES

Aalami, H. A., Moghaddam, P. M., & Yousefi, G. R. (2010). Modeling and Prioritizing Demand Response Programs in Power Markets. *Electric Power Systems Research*, *80*(4), 426–435. doi:10.1016/j.epsr.2009.10.007

Abouelnaga, A. E., Metwally, A., Aly, N., Nagy, M., & Agamy, S. (2010). Assessment of Nuclear Energy Sustainability Index using Fuzzy Logic. *Nuclear Engineering and Design*, *240*(7), 1928–1933. doi:10.1016/j. nucengdes.2010.03.010

Afgan, N. H., Carvalho, M. G., & Hovanov, N. V. (2000). Energy System Assessment with Sustainability Indicators. *Energy Policy*, *28*(9), 603–612. doi:10.1016/S0301-4215(00)00045-8

Afgan, N. H., Carvalho, M. G., & Hovanov, N. V. (2005). Modeling of Energy System Sustainability Index. *Thermal Science*, *9*(2), 3–16. doi:10.2298/ TSCI0502003A

Androulaki, S., Doukas, H., Marinakis, V., Madrazo, L., & Legaki, N. Z. (2016). Enabling Local Authorities to Produce Short-Term Energy Plans: A Multidisciplinary Decision Support Approach. *Management of Environmental Quality*, *27*(2), 146–166. doi:10.1108/MEQ-02-2014-0021

Awasthi, A., & Chauhan, S. S. (2011). Using AHP and Dempster Shafer Theory for Evaluating Sustainable Transport Solutions. *Environmental Modelling & Software*, *26*(6), 787–796. doi:10.1016/j.envsoft.2010.11.010

Balo, F., & Şağbanşua, L. (2016). The Selection of the Best Solar Panel for the Photovoltaic System Design by Using AHP. *Energy Procedia*, *100*, 50–53. doi:10.1016/j.egypro.2016.10.151

Beccali, M., Cellura, M., & Mistretta, M. (2003). Decision-Making in Energy Planning. Application of the Electre method at Regional Level for the Diffusion of Renewable Energy Technology. *Renewable Energy*, *28*(13), 2063–2087. doi:10.1016/S0960-1481(03)00102-2

Bertoldi, P., Cayuela, D. B., Monni, S., & Raveschootm, R. P. (2009). *Existing Methodologies and Tools for the Development and Implementation of Sustainable Energy Action Plans (SEAP). European Commission - Joint Research Centre*. Brussels, Belgium: EC-JRC.

Boran, F. E., Boran, K., & Menlik, T. (2012). The Evaluation of Renewable Energy Technologies for Electricity Generation in Turkey using TOPSIS. *Energy Sources, Part B: Economics, Planning, and Policy*, *7*(1), 81–90. doi:10.1080/15567240903047483

Brown, M. A., & Sovacool, B. K. (2007). Developing an 'Energy Sustainability Index to Evaluate Energy Policy. *Interdisciplinary Science Reviews*, *32*(4), 335–349. doi:10.1179/030801807X211793

Catalina, T., Virgone, J., & Blanco, E. (2011). Multi-Source Energy Systems Analysis Using a Multi-Criteria Decision Aid Methodology. *Renewable Energy*, *36*(8), 2245–2252. doi:10.1016/j.renene.2011.01.011

Cavallaro, F. (2009). Multi-Criteria Decision Aid to Assess Concentrated Solar Thermal Technologies. *Renewable Energy*, *34*(7), 1678–1685. doi:10.1016/j.renene.2008.12.034

Christoforidis, G. C., Chatzisavvas, K. C., Lazarou, S., & Parisses, C. (2013). Covenant of Mayors Initiative-Public Perception Issues and Barriers in Greece. *Energy Policy*, *60*, 643–655. doi:10.1016/j.enpol.2013.05.079

Christoforidis, G. C., Lazarou, S., Parisses, C., & Bakouris, M. (2011). The Covenant of Mayors Initiative: Status in Europe and Barriers towards realizing its Full Potential in Greece. *8th International Conference on the European Energy Market*, 692-697. doi:10.1109/EEM.2011.5953099

CLIMATE COMPASS. (2006). *The CLIMATE COMPASS Compendium of Measures for Local Climate Change Policy*. Author.

CoM – Covenant of Mayors. (2013). *Covenant of Mayors e-learning Course Now Available in Five Languages*. Retrieved October 19, 2016, from: http://www.simfonodimarxon.eu/Covenant-of-Mayors-e-learning,1542.html

CoM - Covenant of Mayors. (2017a). *The Covenant of Mayors for Climate and Energy Reporting Guidelines.* Covenant of Mayors Office & Joint Research Centre of the European Commission. Retrieved January 21, 2017, from: http://www.covenantofmayors.eu/IMG/pdf/Covenant_ReportingGuidelines.pdf

CoM - Covenant of Mayors. (2017b). *Covenant in Figures.* Retrieved January 21, 2017, from: http://www.covenantofmayors.eu/about/covenant-in-figures_en.html

COMBAT. (2008). *COMBAT Report guidelines.* Helsinki, Finland: Author.

CoR - Committee of the Regions. (2014a). *Committee of the Regions' Athens Declaration on the mid-term review of Europe 2020 - a Territorial Vision for Growth and Jobs.* Athens, Greece: Athens Declaration.

CoR - Committee of the Regions. (2014b). Delivering on the Europe 2020 Strategy Handbook for Local and Regional Authorities. Brussels, Belgium: Author.

Covenant CapaCITY. (2013). *Covenant capaCITY Training Platform.* Retrieved November 4, 2016, from: http://www.covenant-capacity.eu/eu/training-platform

CTB - Community Tool Box. (2014). Analyzing Community Problems and Designing and Adapting Community Interventions. In *Deciding Where to Start - Section 2. Participatory Approaches to Planning Community Interventions.* Work Group for Community Health and Development, University of Kansas. Retrieved October 6, 2016, from: http://ctb.ku.edu/en/table-of-contents/analyze/where-to-start/participatory-approaches/main

Deilmann, C., & Bathe, K. J. (2009). A holistic method to design an optimized energy scenario and quantitatively evaluate promising technologies for implementation. *International Journal of Green Energy, 6*(1), 1–21. doi:10.1080/15435070802701702

Demesouka, O.-E., Vavatsikos, A.-P., & Anagnostopoulos, K.-P. (2013). Spatial UTA (S-UTA) – A New Approach for Raster-Based GIS Multicriteria Suitability Analysis and its Use in Implementing Natural Systems for Wastewater Treatment. *Journal of Environmental Management, 125*, 41–54. doi:10.1016/j.jenvman.2013.03.035 PMID:23644589

Domenech, B., Ferrer-Martí, L., & Pastor, R. (2015). Hierarchical Methodology to Optimize the Design of Stand-Alone Electrification Systems for Rural Communities considering Technical and Social Criteria. *Renewable & Sustainable Energy Reviews*, *51*, 182–196. doi:10.1016/j.rser.2015.06.017

Doukas, H., Botsikas, A., & Psarras, J. (2007). Multi-Criteria Decision Aid for the Formulation of Sustainable Technological Energy Priorities using Linguistic Variables. *European Journal of Operational Research*, *182*(2), 844–855. doi:10.1016/j.ejor.2006.08.037

Doukas, H., Karakosta, C., & Psarras, J. (2010). Computing with words to assess the sustainability of renewable energy options. *Expert Systems with Applications*, *37*(7), 5491–5497. doi:10.1016/j.eswa.2010.02.061

Doukas, H., Marinakis, V., & Psarras, J. (2012a). Greening the Hellenic Corporate Energy Policy: An Integrated Decision Support Framework. *International Journal of Green Energy*, *9*(6), 487–502. doi:10.1080/15435075.2011.622023

Doukas, H., Papadopoulou, A., Savvakis, N., Tsoutsos, T., & Psarras, J. (2012b). Assessing Energy Sustainability of Rural Communities using Principal Component Analysis. *Renewable & Sustainable Energy Reviews*, *16*(4), 1949–1957. doi:10.1016/j.rser.2012.01.018

Doukas, H., Tsiousi, A., Marinakis, V., & Psarras, J. (2014). Linguistic Multi-Criteria Decision Making for Energy and Environmental Corporate Policy. *Information Sciences*, *258*, 328–338. doi:10.1016/j.ins.2013.08.027

EC - European Commission. (2006). Communication from the Commission to the Council and the European Parliament: Employment in Rural Areas: Closing the Jobs Gap. COM(2006) 857 final. Brussels, Belgium: EC.

EC - European Commission. (2008). *Communication from the Commission to the European Parliament, the Council, the European Economic and Social Committee and the Committee of the Regions: 20 20 by 2020 Europe's climate change opportunity*. COM (2008) 30 final.

EC - European Commission. (2010a). *A Digital Agenda for Europe*. COM(2010) 245 final.

EC - European Commission. (2010b). *Energy-Efficient Buildings PPP: Multi-Annual Roadmap and Longer Term Strategy*. Directorate-General for Research, Industrial Technologies, prepared by the Ad-hoc Industrial Advisory Group, Brussels, Belgium. Retrieved from http://ec.europa.eu/research/industrial_technologies/pdf/ppp-energy-efficient-building-strategic-multiannual-roadmap-info-day_en.pdf

EC - European Commission. (2010c). *Communication from the Commission Europe 2020 - A strategy for Smart, Sustainable and Inclusive Growth*. COM(2010) 2020 final.

EC - European Commission. (2010d). How to Develop a Sustainable Energy Action Plan (SEAP) – Guidebook. Covenant of Mayors.

EC - European Commission. (2011a). *A resource-efficient Europe – Flagship initiative under the Europe 2020 Strategy*. COM(2011) 21.

EC - European Commission. (2011b). *Communication from the Commission to the European Parliament, the Council, the European Economic and Social Committee and the Committee of the Regions - A Resource-Efficient Europe – Flagship Initiative under the Europe 2020 Strategy*. COM(2011) 21.

EC - European Commission. (2011c). Cities of Tomorrow – Challenges, visions, ways forward. Brussels, Belgium: EC.

EC - European Commission. (2012). *Smart Cities and Communities - European Innovation Partnership*. COM(2012) 4701 final.

EC - European Commission. (2014). *2030 Climate and Energy Framework*. Retrieved February 11, 2017, from: https://ec.europa.eu/clima/policies/strategies/2030_en

EC - European Communities. (2005). *Communication from the Commission to the Council, the European Parliament, the European Economic and Social Committee and the Committee of the Regions: Winning the battle against global climate change. COM(2005) 35 final*. Brussels, Belgium: Commission of the European Communities.

Energie-Cites. (2008). *BELIEF-Involve Stakeholders and Citizens in your Local Energy Turn over a New LIEF!*. Author.

ENNEREG. (2013). Retrieved November 4, 2016, from: http://www.regions202020.eu/cms/sec/ennereg

ENOVA. (2012). *Municipal Energy and Climate Planning – A Guide to the Process*. ENOVA.

ENSRC. (2011). Retrieved November 4, 2016, from: http://www.managenergy. net/resources/921

EPI - Environmental Performance Index. (2015). Retrieved February 12, 2016, from: http://epi.yale.edu

Erol, Ö., & Kılkıs, B. (2012). An Energy Source Policy Assessment using Analytical Hierarchy Process. *Energy Conversion and Management, 63*, 245–252. doi:10.1016/j.enconman.2012.01.040

EU - European Union. (2012). *Rural Development in the EU Statistical and Economic: Information Report 2012*. Brussels, Belgium: Directorate-General for Agriculture and Rural Development.

EU - European Union. (2013). *Delivering on the Europe 2020 Strategy: Handbook for Local and Regional Authorities*. Brussels, Belgium: Committee of the Regions.

European Energy Award. (2007). Cooking Book: CO_2 – Balancing. In *Framework of the Balance Project*. Author.

Evans, A., Strezov, V., & Evans, T. J. (2009). Assessment of Sustainability Indicators for Renewable Energy Technologies. *Renewable & Sustainable Energy Reviews, 13*(5), 1082–1088. doi:10.1016/j.rser.2008.03.008

Figueira, J. R., Greco, S., & Słowinski, R. (2009). Building a Set of Additive Value Functions Representing a Reference Preorder and Intensities of Preference: GRIP Method. *European Journal of Operational Research, 195*(2), 460–486. doi:10.1016/j.ejor.2008.02.006

Fishburn, P. (1966). A Note on Recent Developments in Additive Utility Theories for Multiple Factors Situations. *Operations Research, 14*(6), 1143–1148. doi:10.1287/opre.14.6.1143

Fishburn, P. (1967). Methods for Estimating Additive Utilities. *Management Science, 13*(7), 435–453. doi:10.1287/mnsc.13.7.435

Fliege, J., & Werner, R. (2014). Robust Multiobjective Optimization & Applications in Portfolio Optimization. *European Journal of Operational Research, 234*(2), 422–433. doi:10.1016/j.ejor.2013.10.028

FREE - Future of rural Energy in Europe. (2013). *Rural Myths and Realities*. Retrieved November 4, 2016, from: http://www.rural-energy.eu

Geurts, J. L. A., & Joldersma, C. (2001). Methodology for Participatory Policy Analysis. *European Journal of Operational Research, 128*(2), 300–310. doi:10.1016/S0377-2217(00)00073-4

Ghafghazi, S., Sowlati, T., Sokhansanj, S., & Melin, S. (2010). A Multicriteria Approach to Evaluate District Heating System Options. *Applied Energy, 87*(4), 1134–1140. doi:10.1016/j.apenergy.2009.06.021

Granat, J., & Makowski, M. (2000). Interactive Specification and Analysis of Aspiration-Based Preferences. *European Journal of Operational Research, 122*(2), 469–485. doi:10.1016/S0377-2217(99)00248-9

Greco, S., Mousseau, V., & Słowinski, R. (2008). Ordinal Regression Revisited: Multiple Criteria Ranking Using a set of Additive Value Functions. *European Journal of Operational Research, 191*(2), 416–436. doi:10.1016/j.ejor.2007.08.013

Greco, S., Siskos, Y., & Słowinski, R. (2012). *Controlling Robustness in Ordinal Regression Model*s. Paper presented at the 75th meeting of the EURO working group on MCDA, Tarragona, Spain.

Greening, L. A., & Bernow, S. (2004). Design of Coordinated Energy and Environmental Policies: Use of Multi-Criteria Decision-Making. *Energy Policy, 32*(6), 721–735. doi:10.1016/j.enpol.2003.08.017

Haurant, P., Oberti, P., & Muselli, M. (2011). Multicriteria Selection Aiding Related to Photovoltaic Plants on Farming Fields on Corsica Island: A Real Case Study Using the ELECTRE Outranking Framework. *Energy Policy, 39*(2), 676–688. doi:10.1016/j.enpol.2010.10.040

Hites, R., De Smet, Y., Risse, N., Salazar-Neumann, M., & Vincke, P. (2006). About the Applicability of MCDA to some Robustness Problems. *European Journal of Operational Research, 174*(1), 322–332. doi:10.1016/j.ejor.2005.01.031

ICLEI. (2007). *Climate Protection Manual for Cities*. Natural Capitalism Solutions.

Jun, D., Tian-tian, F., Yi-sheng, Y., & Yu, M. (2014). Macro-site Selection of Wind/Solar Hybrid Power Station based on ELECTRE-II. *Renewable & Sustainable Energy Reviews, 35*, 194–204. doi:10.1016/j.rser.2014.04.005

Kadzinski, M., Greco, S., & Slowinski, R. (2012). Extreme Ranking Analysis in Robust Ordinal Regression. *Omega, 40*(4), 488–501. doi:10.1016/j.omega.2011.09.003

Kadzinski, M., Greco, S., & Slowinski, R. (2013). RUTA: A Framework for Assessing and Selecting Additive Value Functions on the basis of Rank Related Requirements. *Omega, 41*(3), 735–751. doi:10.1016/j.omega.2012.10.002

Kadzinski, M., & Tervonen, T. (2013a). Stochastic Ordinal Regression for Multiple Criteria Sorting Problems. *Decision Support Systems, 55*(1), 55–66. doi:10.1016/j.dss.2012.12.030

Kadzinski, M., & Tervonen, T. (2013b). Robust Multi-Criteria Ranking with Additive Value Models and Holistic Pair-Wise Preference Statements. *European Journal of Operational Research, 228*(1), 169–180. doi:10.1016/j.ejor.2013.01.022

Kalbar, P. P., Karmakar, S., & Asolekar, S. R. (2012). Selection of an Appropriate Wastewater Treatment Technology: A Scenario-Based Multiple-Attribute Decision-Making Approach. *Journal of Environmental Management, 113*, 158–169. doi:10.1016/j.jenvman.2012.08.025 PMID:23023038

Kambezidis, H., Kasselouri, B., & Konidari, P. (2011). Evaluating Policy Options for Increasing the RES-E Penetration in Greece. *Energy Policy, 39*(9), 5388–5398. doi:10.1016/j.enpol.2011.05.025

Keeney, R. L., & Raiffa, H. (1976). *Decisions with Multiple Objectives: Preferences and Value Tradeoffs*. New York: John Wiley and Sons.

Kholghi, M. (2001). Multi-Criterion Decision-Making Tools for Wastewater Planning Management. *Journal of Agricultural Science and Technology, 3*, 281–286.

Koepper, J., Pavese, N., Gonzalez, I. A., & Birnstill, M. (2009). *A CSR Europe Helpdesk Service: Integration of CSR/Sustainable Development into Performance Assessments and Evaluation Processes at Large Companies*. Brussels, Belgium: CSR Europe.

Kowalski, K., Stagl, S., Madlener, R., & Omann, I. (2009). Sustainable Energy Futures: Methodological Challenges in Combining Scenarios and Participatory Multi-Criteria Analysis. *European Journal of Operational Research, 197*(3), 1063–1074. doi:10.1016/j.ejor.2007.12.049

Kuang, H., Marc Kilgour, D., & Hipel, K. W. (2015). Grey-based PROMETHEE II with application to evaluation of source water protection strategies. *Information Sciences, 294*, 376–389. doi:10.1016/j.ins.2014.09.035

Lanjewar, P. B., Rao, R. V., & Kale, A. V. (2015). Assessment of Alternative Fuels for Transportation using a Hybrid Graph Theory and Analytic Hierarchy Process Method. *Fuel, 154*(15), 9–16. doi:10.1016/j.fuel.2015.03.062

Lee, W.-S., & Lin, L.-C. (2011). Evaluating and Ranking the Energy Performance of Office Building Using Technique for Order Preference by Similarity to Ideal Solution. *Applied Thermal Engineering, 31*(16), 3521–3525. doi:10.1016/j.applthermaleng.2011.07.005

Lund, H. (2007). Renewable Energy Strategies for Sustainable Development. *Energy, 32*(6), 912–919. doi:10.1016/j.energy.2006.10.017

Madlener, R., Kowalski, K., & Stagl, S. (2007). New Ways for the Integrated Appraisal of National Energy Scenarios: The Case of Renewable Energy Use in Austria. *Energy Policy, 35*(12), 6060–6074. doi:10.1016/j.enpol.2007.08.015

MAKE-IT-BE. (2011). *Decision Making and Implementation Tools for Delivery of Local & Regional BioEnergy Chains*. Author.

Marinakis, V., Doukas, H., Xidonas, P., & Zopounidis, C. (2017). Multicriteria Decision Support in Local Energy Planning: An Evaluation of Alternative Scenarios for the Sustainable Energy Action Plan. *Omega – The International Journal of Management Science*.

Marinakis, V., Papadopoulou, A., Doukas, H., & Psarras, J. (2015). A Web Tool for Sustainable Energy Communities. *International Journal of Information and Decision Sciences, 7*(1), 18–31. doi:10.1504/IJIDS.2015.068115

Marinakis, V., Papadopoulou, A., & Psarras, J. (2012). Strengthening Sustainable Energy Policies within the Covenant of Mayors Initiative. *Proceedings of the 5th International Scientific Conference on "Energy and Climate Change"*.

Marinakis, V., Papadopoulou, A., & Psarras, J. (2017). Local Communities towards a Sustainable Energy Future: Needs and Priorities. *International Journal of Sustainable Energy, 36*(3), 296–312. doi:10.1080/14786451.2015.1018264

Marinakis, V., Papadopoulou, A., Siskos, J., & Psarras, J. (2012). Sustainable Energy Communities: A Methodological Framework for the Support of Local and Regional Stakeholders. *Proceedings of the 23rd National Conference of the Hellenic Operational Research Society (HELORS)*.

Mavrotas, G., Figueira, J. R., & Siskos, E. (2015). Robustness Analysis Methodology for Multi-Objective Combinatorial Optimization Problems and Application to Project Selection. *Omega*, *52*, 142–155. doi:10.1016/j.omega.2014.11.005

Meyar-Naimin, H., & Vaez-Zadeh, S. (2012). Sustainable Development Based Energy Policy Making Frameworks, A Critical Review. *Energy Policy*, *43*, 351–361. doi:10.1016/j.enpol.2012.01.012

Minnesota Project, University of Minnesota's Regional, Sustainable Development Partnerships, Minnesota Department of Commerce. (2003). *Designing A Clean Energy Future: A Resource Manual – Developed for the Clean Energy Resources Teams*. Author.

MODEL. (2008). *Common Framework Methodology (CFM) for Municipal Energy Planning*. MODEL.

Mousavi, M., Gitinavard, H., & Mousavi, S. M. (2017). A soft computing based-modified ELECTRE model for renewable energy policy selection with unknown information. *Renewable & Sustainable Energy Reviews*, *68*(1), 774–787. doi:10.1016/j.rser.2016.09.125

Moving Sustainably Project. (2011). *Moving Sustainably - Guide to Sustainable Urban Transport Plans*. Author.

Munda, G. (2004). Social Multi-Criteria Evaluation: Methodological Foundations and Operational Consequences. *European Journal of Operational Research*, *158*(3), 662–677. doi:10.1016/S0377-2217(03)00369-2

MUSEC. (2007). *Energy Baseline Assessment and Target-Setting*. Guidelines for Energy Accounting Procedure.

Niemeijer, D., & de Groot, R. (2007). A Conceptual Framework for Selecting Environmental Indicator Sets. *Ecological Indicators*, *8*(1), 14–25. doi:10.1016/j.ecolind.2006.11.012

Nowak, M. (2007). Aspiration Level Approach in Stochastic MCDM Problems. *European Journal of Operational Research*, *177*(3), 1626–1640. doi:10.1016/j.ejor.2005.10.003

OECD. (2002). *Aggregated Environmental Indices: Review of Aggregation Methodologies in Use*. OECD.

Omer, A. M. (2008). Energy, Environment and Sustainable Development. *Renewable & Sustainable Energy Reviews, 12*(9), 2265–2300. doi:10.1016/j. rser.2007.05.001

Oxfam International. (2007). *Adapting to climate change: What's needed in poor countries and who should pay*. Retrieved March 10, 2011, from: http:// www.oxfam.org/sites/www.oxfam.org/files/adapting%20to%20climate%20 change.pdf

Özkan, A., Banar, M., Acar, I., & Sipahioğlu, A. (2011). Application of the ELECTRE III Method for a Solid Waste Management System. *Applied Sciences and Engineering, 12*(1), 11–23.

Pan, J., Teklu, Y., Rahman, S., & de Castro, A. (2000). An Interval-Based MADM Approach to the Identification of Candidate Alternatives in Strategic Resource Planning. *IEEE Transactions on Power Systems, 15*(4), 1441–1446. doi:10.1109/59.898125

Papadopoulos, A., & Karagiannidis, A. (2008). Application of the Multi-Criteria Analysis Method Electre III for the Optimisation of Decentralised Energy Systems. *Omega, 36*(5), 766–776. doi:10.1016/j.omega.2006.01.004

PEPESEC. (2008). *Energy Planning Guidance – PEPESEC Project*. Author.

Polatidis, H., & Haralambopoulos, D. A. (2004). Local Renewable Energy Planning: A Participatory Multi-Criteria Approach. *Energy Sources, 26*(13), 1253–1264. doi:10.1080/00908310490441584

Porter, M. E. (1990). The Competitive Advantage of Nations. *Harvard Business Review*. Retrieved November 19, 2016, from: https://hbr.org/1990/03/the-competitive-advantage-of-nations

Rees, H., Hyland, J., Hylland, K., Mercer Clarke, C., Roff, J., & Ware, S. (2008). Environmental Indicators: Utility in Meeting Regulatory Needs. An Overview. *ICES Journal of Marine Science, 65*(8), 1381–1386. doi:10.1093/ icesjms/fsn153

Renn, O., Webler, T., Rakel, H., Dienel, P., & Johnson, B. (1993). Public Participation in Decision Making: A Three Step Procedure. *Policy Sciences, 26*(3), 189–214. doi:10.1007/BF00999716

100.   RES-COMMUNITIES. (2010). Retrieved December 18, 2015, from http://eaci-projects.eu/iee/page/Page.jsp?op=project_detail&prid=2550

Rojas-Zerpa, J. C., & Yusta, J. M. (2014). Methodologies, Technologies and Applications for Electric Supply Planning in Rural Remote Areas. *Energy for Sustainable Development*, *20*, 66–76. doi:10.1016/j.esd.2014.03.003

Roy, B. (2010). Robustness in Operational Research and Decision Aiding: A Multi-Faceted Issue. *European Journal of Operational Research*, *200*(3), 629–638. doi:10.1016/j.ejor.2008.12.036

SEC-Tools. (2008). *Promotion of Sustainable Energy Practice at Community level in EU*. Author.

SECURE Project. (2008). *Finding Your Way to Energy Actions – Guidelines for Communities on How to Set an Energy Action Plan*. Author.

Shen, Y.-C., Chou, C. J., & Lin, G. T. R. (2011). The Portfolio of Renewable Energy Sources for Achieving the Three Policy Goals. *Energy*, *36*(5), 2589–2598. doi:10.1016/j.energy.2011.01.053

Sindhu, S. P., Nehra, V., & Luthra, S. (2016). Recognition and prioritization of challenges in growth of solar energy using analytical hierarchy process: Indian outlook. *Energy*, *100*, 332–348. doi:10.1016/j.energy.2016.01.091

Siskos, E., & Tsotsolas, N. (2015). Elicitation of Criteria Importance Weights through the Simos Method: A Robustness Concern. *European Journal of Operational Research*, *246*(2), 543–553. doi:10.1016/j.ejor.2015.04.037

Siskos, Y. (2001). Preference Disaggregation. In Encyclopedia of Optimization (pp. 2003-2014). doi:10.1007/0-306-48332-7_394

Sola, A.-V.-H., & Mota, C. M. M. (2012). A Multi-Attribute Decision Model for Portfolio Selection Aiming to Replace Technologies in Industrial Motor Systems. *Energy Conversion and Management*, *57*, 97–106. doi:10.1016/j.enconman.2011.12.013

Stagl, S. (2007). *Emerging Methods for Sustainability Valuation and Appraisal – SDRN Rapid Research and Evidence Review*. Sustainable Development Research Network. Retrieved November 4, 2016, from: http://www.sd-research.org.uk

Stern, N. (2007). *The economics of climate change: The Stern Review*. Cambridge, UK: Cambridge University Press. doi:10.1017/CBO9780511817434

Stigson, P., Dotzauer, E., & Yan, J. (2009). Climate and energy policy evaluation in terms of relative industrial performance and competitiveness. *International Journal of Green Energy*, *6*(5), 450–465. doi:10.1080/15435070903227953

Tegou, I., Polatidis, H., & Haralambopoulos, D. A. (2010). Environmental Management Framework for Wind Farm Siting: Methodology and Case Study. *Journal of Environmental Management*, *91*(11), 2134–2147. doi:10.1016/j.jenvman.2010.05.010 PMID:20541310

Terrados, J., Almonacid, G., & Perez-Higueras, P. (2009). Proposal for a Combined Methodology for Renewable Energy Planning – Application to a Spanish Region. *Renewable & Sustainable Energy Reviews*, *13*(8), 2022–2030. doi:10.1016/j.rser.2009.01.025

TMCE - Toolbox of Methodologies on Climate and Energy. (2011). Retrieved from http://toolbox.climate-protection.eu

TMCE - Toolbox of Methodologies on Climate and Energy. (2013). *Guidance for Local Governments and their Partners: Toolbox of Methodologies on Climate and Energy*. Retrieved December 18, 2015, from: http://toolbox.climate-protection.eu/

Tsoutsos, Th., Drandaki, M., Frantzeskaki, N., Iosifidis, E., & Kiosses, I. (2009). Sustainable Energy Planning by Using Multi-Criteria Analysis Application in the Island of Crete. *Energy Policy*, *37*(5), 1587–1600. doi:10.1016/j.enpol.2008.12.011

UNDP (United Nations Development Programme). (2007). *Human Development Report 2007/2008: Fighting climate change—Human solidarity in a divided world*. New York: Palgrave Macmillan.

UNFCCC (United Nations Framework Convention on Climate Change). (2007). *Report on the analysis of existing and potential investment and financial flows relevant to the development of an effective and appropriate international response to climate change*. Retrieved from http://unfccc.int/files/cooperation_and_support/financial_mechanism/financial_mechanism_gef/application/pdf/dialogue_working_paper_8.pdf

Vera, I., & Langlois, L. (2007). Energy Indicators for Sustainable Development. *Energy, 32*(6), 875–882. doi:10.1016/j.energy.2006.08.006

Volvačiovas, R., Turskis, Z., Aviža, D., & Mikštienė, R. (2013). Multi-attribute Selection of Public Buildings Retrofits Strategy. *Procedia Engineering, 57*, 1236–1241. doi:10.1016/j.proeng.2013.04.156

Voropai, N. L., & Ivanova, E. Y. (2002). Multicriteria Decision Analysis Technique in Electric Power System Expansion Planning. *Electrical Power and Energy Systems, 24*(1), 71–78. doi:10.1016/S0142-0615(01)00005-9

Wang, J., & Zionts, S. (2006). The Aspiration Level Interactive Method (AIM) Reconsidered: Robustness of Solutions. *European Journal of Operational Research, 175*(2), 948–958. doi:10.1016/j.ejor.2005.06.039

Wang, J.-J., Jing, Y.-Y., Zhang, C.-F., & Zhao, J.-H. (2009). Review on Multi-Criteria Decision Analysis Aid in Sustainable Energy Decision-Making. *Renewable & Sustainable Energy Reviews, 13*(9), 2263–2278. doi:10.1016/j.rser.2009.06.021

Wise Plans. (2007). Retrieved November 4, 2016, from: http://www.wiseplans.eu

World Bank. (2009). *World Development Report 2010: Development and climate change*. Washington, DC: World Bank.

Yun, Y. B., Nakayama, H., & Arakawa, M. (2004). Multiple Criteria Decision Making with generalized DEA and an aspiration Level Method. *European Journal of Operational Research, 158*(3), 697–706. doi:10.1016/S0377-2217(03)00375-8

ENDNOTE

[1] The CoM initiative is a voluntary agreement of the municipalities to go beyond the EU objectives in terms of CO_2 emission reduction. Available at http://www.eumayors.eu/index_en.html.

Chapter 2
Making Sustainable Energy Communities a Reality:
The "MPC⁺" Decision Support Framework

ABSTRACT

The aim of this chapter is to present a decision support framework for local energy planning, entitled "MPC⁺ (Map - Plan - Choose - Check)". The proposed framework incorporates the development of the baseline emissions inventory, the identification and modelling of renewable energy and rational use of energy actions, as well as the creation of alternative Scenarios of Actions at the city level. The evaluation of alternative Scenarios is based on a multi-criteria ordinal regression approach. In addition, an extreme ranking analysis method is used, in order to examine robustness problems, estimating the best and worst possible ranking position of each Scenario. The MPC⁺ framework contributes to the selection of the most promising Scenario of renewable energy and rational use of energy actions, supporting the local - regional authorities in creating Sustainable Energy Communities (SEC). Finally, the "Methodological Approach for Monitoring SEC Targets" is introduced.

DOI: 10.4018/978-1-5225-2286-7.ch002

INTRODUCTION

This chapter presents a decision support framework for local energy planning. The overall philosophy of the proposed framework aims to support the local and regional authorities in the development, implementation and monitoring of the Sustainable Energy and Climate Action Plan, especially within the framework of the Covenant of Mayors' initiative. More specifically, the proposed framework "MPC+ (Map - Plan - Choose - Check)" integrates the following four components:

- **"Map":** This component is the starting point of the Action Plan's development process. It involves the mapping of the current status within the region, emphasizing on the development of energy and baseline emission inventory. The results at this stage are the basis for the formulation of a comprehensive Action Plan and the monitoring and control of targets set.
- **"Plan":** This component focuses on the design of alternative Scenarios of Actions, namely a set of appropriate measures and actions for implementation at local - regional level. The design of scenarios is achieved through the modeling of measures and actions, the assessment of future trends in CO_2 emissions at local - regional level and the participation of local stakeholders.
- **"Choose":** This component aims to support decision makers in the process of identifying the most promising Scenario of Actions for the region. It includes the evaluation of the alternative Scenarios of Actions using multi-criteria analysis and robustness analysis.
- **"Check":** This component is related to the monitoring of the targets set in each activity sector of the municipality. In this way, the monitoring and assessment of the progress towards sustainable development in economic, social and environmental context is achieved.

Apart from the introduction, the paper is structured along six sections. Section 2 provides a description of the overall technical framework of the proposed "MPC+" approach. Sections 3-6 are devoted to the presentation of the four components of the proposed approach, namely "Map", "Plan", "Choose" and "Check" components. Finally, the last section just summarizes the key issues that have arisen in this paper.

Technical Framework

The proposed framework includes individual components, which are described below (Figure 1):

- **"Map" Component:**
  - ○ **Baseline Year:** Selection of the year for which the energy and emission baseline inventory will be developed.

Figure 1. Algorithm of the proposed decision making framework

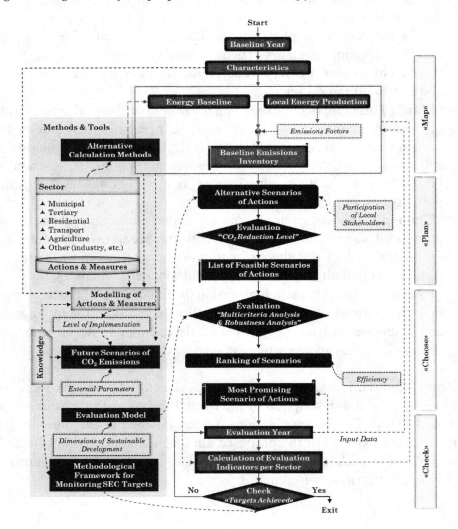

- ◦ **Characteristics:** Some basic information and statistics are required for the municipality (e.g. population, number of dwellings, land uses, etc.). These data are used both in the development of energy and emission baseline, as well as in the design of alternative Scenarios of Actions.
- ◦ **Energy Balance:** Calculation of energy balance at the local-regional level with the use of alternative methods.
- ◦ **Local Energy Production:** Data on the local electricity production and local heating / cooling systems. These data are used for the calculation of regional CO_2 emission factors.
- ◦ **Baseline Emissions Inventory:** The last stage includes the development of the baseline emission inventory, taking into consideration the energy balance and emission factors per energy use (national and local).
- **"Plan" Component:**
  - ◦ **Actions' Modelling:** First of all, a number of renewable energy and rational use of energy actions have been identified for the following sectors, as proposed by the Covenant of Mayors' guidelines (CoM, 2017):
    - ▪ Agricultural/fishery/forestry sector;
    - ▪ Municipal buildings, equipment/facilities (public, tertiary and residential);
    - ▪ Transport (municipal fleet, public transport, private and commercial transport);
    - ▪ Local electricity production (hydroelectric power, wind power, photovoltaic, combined heat and power, etc.);
      Local district heating/cooling (combined heat and power, district heating plant, etc.).

    These actions take an "editable" form using data provided by decision-maker (community's profile, baseline energy and CO_2 emission inventory), as well as indicators from the international literature and reports.
  - ◦ **Scenarios' Development:** An initial design of alternative scenarios takes place according to the range of the actions' application in each sector. The appropriate modifications are made on these scenarios through a participatory approach (using questionnaires, public consultation meeting, etc.).

- ○ **Evaluation (Level of CO$_2$ Emissions Reduction):** All the alternative scenarios are evaluated concerning the reduction of CO$_2$ emissions, based on the threshold set by the local authorities (e.g. 20% by 2020 or 40% by 2030).
- ○ **List Feasible Scenarios of Actions:** Creation of the list of feasible Scenarios, which will be evaluated subsequently in order to identify the most promising scenario to be implemented by the region.

- **"Choose" Component:**
  - ○ **Evaluation (Multicriteria Decision Support and Robustness Analysis):** The alternative scenarios are evaluated through the construction of a coherent family of criteria and an evaluation model. An Additive Value Function is used for the assessment of the alternatives scenarios. Linear programming techniques used in conjunction with qualitative regression analysis (Multicriteria Ordinal Regression Approach). The extreme ranking analysis method is used, in order to take into account the model's robustness, estimating the best and worst possible ranking position of each scenario.
  - ○ **Ranking of Alternative Scenarios of Actions:** Based on the above approach, the final ranking of alternative Scenarios of Actions is derived, reflecting the maximum and minimum position of each Scenario. In this respect, the most promising Scenario of Actions can be identified taking also into consideration the relevant efficiency.

- **"Check" Component:**
  - ○ **Evaluation Year:** For the elected evaluation year, the relevant data for the baseline emission inventory and the progress on actions and measures implementation are introduced.
  - ○ **Calculation of Monitoring Indicators in Each Activity Sector:** Based on the data input, the calculation of the monitoring indicators in each activity sector take place.
  - ○ **Check (Targets Achieved):** Calculation of the composite index "SEC$_{Index}$" in each activity sector, in order to evaluate the overall progress and facilitate the identification of deviations and corrective measures needed.

"MAP" COMPONENT

Baseline Year

According to the Covenant's guidelines, the recommended baseline year is 1990, but if the local authority does not have data to compile a CO_2 inventory for 1990, then it should choose the closest subsequent year for which the most comprehensive and reliable data can be collected.

Characteristics

The end-user provides data regarding general characteristics of the municipality, as follows:

- **General Information:** Population; area; climate zone; employment.
- **Agricultural Sector:** Cultivate land; number of tractors; irrigation methods.
- **Municipal Sector:** Number of municipal buildings; type and total area; number and type of pumps, drillings, water tanks, biological treatment
- **Residential Sector:** Number of buildings and area; buildings with or without central heating; detached houses or block of apartments.
- **Tertiary Sector:** Number buildings, types and area
- **Municipal Lighting:** Number and type of lights
- **Transport:** Number of municipal cars, buses and other vehicles; number of private passenger vehicles, motorcycles, trucks, etc.
- **Locally Energy Production:** Solar radiation; wind speed; river area and flow.

Energy Baseline: Alternative Calculation Methods

A common technical approach has been adopted, as well as the necessary algorithms for the calculations of the energy and CO_2 emissions baseline have been developed. It should be noted that specific emphasis has been given in the sectors of agriculture, forestry and fishery, taking into consideration that these sectors constitute an important part of the baseline emission inventory of the city. The main aim is to facilitate the calculation of energy consumption per sector (especially for tertiary sector, residential buildings, private and commercial transport, agriculture, etc.), providing alternative calculation methods to the users.

Indeed, the approach used for the data entry regarding all buildings and facilities' energy consumptions is either based on existing aggregated data for a specific type of facilities (e.g. schools), either on the bottom up approach and/or use of appropriate estimations where considered necessary (Figure 2).

Buildings, Equipment/Facilities and Industries

- Municipal Buildings/Equipment/Facilities.
  - Schools.
    - Total energy consumption (aggregated data).
    - Bottom up approach - Individual energy consumptions for Nursery schools, Primary schools, Lower secondary schools, Upper secondary schools etc.
  - Municipal Buildings.
    - Total energy consumption (aggregated data).
    - Bottom up approach - Individual energy consumptions for Community Offices, Hospitals, Sports Facilities, Culture Buildings, Other.

Figure 2. Energy baseline: Alternative calculation methods

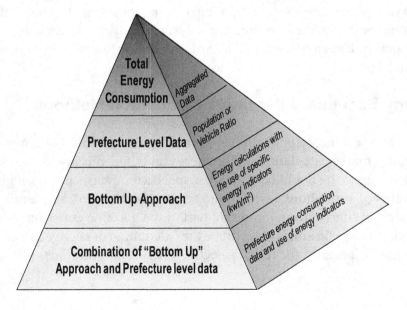

- ○ Equipments/Facilities.
  - ▪ Total energy consumption (aggregated data).
  - ▪ Bottom up approach - Individual energy consumptions for Water treatment units, Recycling centres, Composting plants, Sewage treatment, Other.
- Tertiary (non Municipal) Buildings, Equipment/Facilities.
  - ○ Total energy consumption (aggregated data).
  - ○ Energy consumption at district level (estimation based on population ratio).
    - ▪ Energy consumption at district level, calculation of the municipality consumption based on the population of community and district ratio.
  - ○ Estimations using the bottom up approach for each building category (e.g. Offices, Stores, Hotels, Hospitals, Other).
    - ▪ **Electricity Consumption Estimation:** Based on the number and area (m^2) of buildings for each category, use of average electricity consumption indicators for each building category (kWh/m^2).
    - ▪ **Space Heating:** Estimations based on: number and area (m^2) of buildings per building category, number (or percentage) of buildings with thermal insulation per building category, average energy consumption for heating per m^2 and building category, indicators regarding the % of each fuel (e.g. diesel, electricity, natural gas, biomass etc) in the heating energy mix.
    - ▪ District heating aggregated data (from the suppliers).
    - ▪ **Water Heating :** Solar collectors (Solar collectors' installation - m^2 and energy saving through solar collectors - KWh/m^2 for each country).
- Residential Buildings.
  - ○ Total energy consumption (aggregated data).
  - ○ Energy consumption at district level (estimation based on population or building square meters' ratio).
    - ▪ Energy consumption at district level, calculation of the residential consumption based on the community/ district population or building square meters' ratio.
  - ○ Individual energy consumptions.
    - ▪ **Electricity Consumption:** Estimation and bottom up approach based on the number and area (m^2) of detached

houses and block of apartments and average electricity consumption in buildings (kWh/m^2). The electricity consumption may or may not include consumption for space heating (depending on the availability of indicator data).

- **Space Heating:** Estimations and bottom up approach based on: area (m^2) and number of detached houses and apartments blocks with and without central heating; number of buildings with thermal insulation, for the categories with and without central heating; average energy consumption for heating (kWh/m^2), for buildings with and without central heating; indicators regarding the % of each fuel (e.g. diesel, natural gas, electricity, etc) in the heating energy mix; especially for biomass, indicators for the average use of fuelwood (tons per household) and number of households are used.
- District heating aggregated data (from the suppliers).
- **Water Heating:** Solar collectors (Solar collectors' installation - m^2 and energy saving through solar collectors - KWh/m^2 for each country).

- Public Lighting.
  - Total energy consumption (aggregated data).
  - **Bottom up Approach:** Individual energy consumptions based on the location and relevant energy consumption (kWh per location).
- Industries (excluding industries involved in the EU Emission trading scheme - ETS):
  - Total energy consumption - (aggregated data).
  - Estimations based on the energy consumption at district level and use of ratio.

Transport

- Municipal fleet.
  - Total energy consumption (aggregated data).
  - Bottom up approach from the individual energy consumptions based on:
    - Vehicle Type (Road Grader, Excavator, Bus, Pickup Truck, Garbage Truck, Ambulance, Car, Fire Brigade truck),
    - Number of vehicle and km,
    - Average fuel consumption and fuel type.

- Public transport.
    - ○ Total energy consumption (aggregated data).
    - ○ Bottom up approach from the individual energy consumptions based on:
        - ▪ Bus Route (number of km and number of routes per year).
        - ▪ Average fuel consumption and fuel type.
- Private and commercial transport.
    - ○ Total energy consumption (aggregated data)
    - ○ Estimations based on the energy consumption at district level and use of community/ district population or vehicle ratio.
    - ○ Bottom up approach from the individual energy consumptions based on:
        - ▪ Number of vehicles, motorcycles and vehicles for transport of goods.
        - ▪ Average energy consumption of each type of vehicle.
- Other transportation.
    - ○ Total energy consumption (aggregated data).

Agriculture - Forestry - Fishery

- Agriculture.
    - ○ Electricity (irrigation).
        - ▪ Total energy consumption (aggregated data).
        - ▪ Approximate energy consumption - Water Use (m^3) and relevant indicators (kWh/m^3).
    - ○ Petroleum consumption (agricultural products).
        - ▪ Total energy consumption (aggregated data).
        - ▪ **Estimated Energy Consumption – 1st Method:** Agricultural area for each product (cotton, wheat, maize etc – Ha) and relevant energy consumption indicators (kWh/Ha).
        - ▪ **Estimated Energy Consumption – 2nd Method:** Total agricultural area, power of tractors (kW) and operation Hours (machine-hours/Ha), as well as average energy consumption.
- Forestry.
    - ○ Total energy consumption for the gathering and production of one ton of biomass (based on national studies).
- Fishery.
    - ○ Total energy consumption (aggregated data).

   ○   Estimated energy consumption based on:
- Number of the coastal fishing boats,
- Average power of boats,
- Annual operation hours,
- Average energy consumption.

Other Emissions

- Total energy consumption (aggregated data).

Local Energy Production

Data are required about the thermal power stations operating in the examined municipality, in order to produce electricity. According to the Covenant's guidelines, the end-user should include a project in the baseline emission inventory only if the installed capacity is below 20MW. In this respect, for a group of small (<20MW) similar projects the proposed approach gives the option of adding a group of projects as one only if the installed capacity of each one of the projects participating in the group is below or equal to 20 MW.

In addition, all the currently operating renewable energy and rational use of energy projects in the municipality are taken into consideration. It works exactly the same way like before as far as the projects' grouping is concerned but now there are some differences depending the projects' category. In case the project concerns wind power or hydroelectric or photovoltaic, then the end-user should fill in the fields precisely as in the previous step with the slight exception that now, the end-user does not have to fill in the energy carrier input since this info is now not applicable. If the project relates to combined heat and power units there is a small differentiation, since now the end-user has to fill in separately the data for the power produced and the heat produced (Figure 3).

Baseline Emission Inventory

Two different approaches have been proposed to calculate the energy balance analysis of the region and to identify the principal sources of CO_2 emissions, as well as their respective reduction potentials. The first method considers the "standard" emission factors according to the Intergovernmental Panel

Figure 3. Local energy production

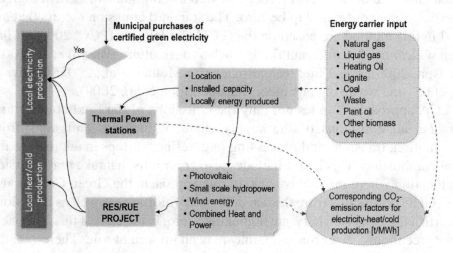

on Climate Change (IPCC) principles (IPCC, 2006), whilst the latter one considers the Life Cycle Assessment (LCA) emission factors (Table 1).

The IPCC method covers all the CO_2 emissions that occur due to energy consumption within the territory of the local authority, either directly due to fuel combustion within the local authority or indirectly via fuel combustion associated with electricity and heat/cold usage within their area. The standard emission factors that are used in this method are based on the carbon content of each fuel and it is assumed that all carbon in the fuel forms CO_2. In this approach, CO_2 is the most important greenhouse gas, and the emissions of CH_4 and N_2O are not calculated. Furthermore, the CO_2 emissions from the

Table 1. Emissions factors

Fuel	IPCC (tnCO$_2$/MWh)	LCA (tnCO$_2$-eq/MWh)
Gasoline	0.249	0.299
Diesel	0.267	0.305
Lignite	0.364	0.375
Natural gas	0.202	0.237
Biomass	0 – 0.403	0.002 – 0.405
Biodiesel	0	0.156
Solar heating	0	-
Geothermal	0	-

sustainable use of biomass/biofuels, as well as emissions of certified green electricity, are considered to be zero. The standard emission factors that are used in this method are based on the IPCC Guidelines (IPCC, 2006). It has been widely used in different fields, such as agriculture (Brown et al., 2001; Nevison, 2000), fossil fuel technologies (La Mottaa et al., 2005; Olivier et al., 2005) and waste management (Papageorgiou et al., 2009).

LCA approach includes not only the emissions of the final combustion, but also all emissions of the supply chain. It includes emissions from exploitation, transport and processing (e.g. refinery) steps in addition to the final combustion. This hence includes also emissions that take place outside the location where the fuel is used. In this approach, the Green Greenhouse Gas (GHG) emissions from the use of biomass/biofuels, as well as emissions of certified green electricity, are higher than zero. In the case of this approach, other greenhouse gases than CO_2 may play an important role. Therefore, the local authority that decides to use the LCA approach can report emissions as CO_{2-eq}.

LCA method has been widely used in different sectors, such as fossil fuel and renewable energy technologies (Sobrinoa et al.,2011; Martíneza et al., 2010; Weisser, 2007; Dones et al., 2004; Varun, et al., 2009; Cherubinia et al., 2009; Babusiaux et al., 2007; Lenzen et al., 2004; Góralczyk, 2003; Pehnt, 2006; Masruroh et al., 2006; Ardente et al., 2005; Ardente et al., 2005; Khan et al., 2005; Martínez et al., 2009), waste management (Ozeler et al., 2006; Borghi et al., 2005; Björklund et al., 2003), as well as construction industry (Ortiza et al., 2009; Erlandssona et al., 2003; Zabalza Bribián et al., 2009), communication systems (Emmenegger M.F et al., 2004) and food products (Poritosh et al., 2009).

Based on the emission factors (national and/or local), the inventory quantifies the amount of CO_2 emitted due to energy consumption in the territory of the Covenant signatory.

"PLAN" COMPONENT

Actions and Measures

The proposed approach includes the development of alternative Scenarios though a knowledge-based process. More specifically, based on desktop analysis (experience, studies, reports, best practices, etc.), different renewable energy and rational use of energy actions for the local authorities, as well as interventions for the local population have been identified (Table 2).

Creation of Scenarios of Actions

Following the identification of renewable energy and rational use of energy actions, there is the need for a modelling process, so as all the proposed actions to take an "editable" form. In this way, the development of alternative scenarios is possible. To this end, all the factors that affect the final energy saving and production from the implementation of these actions have to be identified.

The implementation of all the proposed actions from the local authorities cannot be feasible at economical and organizational level, taking into consideration that each municipality has different characteristics in terms of population, infrastructures, construction of buildings, etc. In this respect, a number of alternative scenarios are created. The scenarios includes different range of application of each action in the relevant sectors, approaching the real needs and opportunities of each municipality, as possible. This means that there are scenarios with emphasis on the residential and/or tertiary sector, other scenarios focused on actions from the local authorities (e.g. municipal buildings, equipment/facilities and public lighting), etc.

Figure 4 depicts a qualitative representation of the range of application in each sector for the initial design of alternative Scenarios. The selection of the range was based on the experience from the development and elaboration of the Sustainable Energy and Climate Action Plans within the framework of the Covenant's initiative, as well as other related activities, such as the Intelligent Energy Europe (IEE) programme.

Future Estimated Progress of the Consumptions and CO_2 Reductions

The proposed model integrates data from the final energy consumption of each sector for the baseline year, a number of external key parameters, as well as the expected energy and CO_2 emissions reduction from the application of examined renewable energy and rational use of energy actions. The adopted approach for the development of the proposed model was based on experts' engagement though the Delphi method. The Delphi Method includes a structured process for collecting and distilling knowledge from a group of experts by means of a

Table 2. Sectors' and actions' identification

Sector	Actions by the Local Authorities	Interventions by the Local Population
S_1 - Agricultural/ Fishery/ Forestry Sector	A_{11} Establishment/adjustment of a Department for Rural Development in the municipality. A_{12} Training seminars regarding the agricultural tractors' modernization and irrigation techniques. A_{13} Implementation of wide informational campaign. A_{14} Installation of an electronic water-supply system for irrigation based on debit cards.	I_{11} Modernization and replacement of tractors. I_{12} Replacement of surface irrigation and sprinkler irrigation with drip irrigation.
S_2 - Municipal Buildings, Equipment/ Facilities	A_{21} Energy certification and improvement of the municipal buildings' energy performance. A_{22} Actions and campaigns for awareness raising of municipal employees. A_{23} Improvement of the school buildings' energy performance. A_{24} Actions and campaigns for awareness raising of pupils and students. A_{25} Energy Management System (in accordance with the ISO 50001). A_{26} Improvement of the sports facilities' energy performance. A_{27} Improvement of the energy performance of the water system and sewage treatment facilities. A_{28} Establishment of the Energy Efficiency Department in the Municipality. A_{29} Appointment of the municipality energy manager. A_{210} Remote configuration and control of the water system.	Not applicable
S_3 - Residential & Tertiary Sector	A_{31} Implementation of campaigns, events, energy days for the citizens. A_{32} Design and distribution of brochures about the benefits of interventions in the residential buildings. A_{33} Targeted seminars to professional groups. A_{34} Initiatives to support the citizens' actions. A_{35} Energy efficiency criteria for the purchase of electrical appliances	I_{31} Improvement of the building envelope (thermal insulation of walls, windows, roofs; external shading). I_{32} Retrofitting of residential buildings, bundling together technology improvements (lighting, electrical equipment, heat/cold systems, etc.). I_{33} Deployment of smart meters in households. I_{34} Installation of BEMs in commercial buildings.
S_4 - Public Lighting	A_{41} Gradual replacement of the existing bulbs in the public lighting with more efficient ones. A_{42} Dimmers depending on ambient conditions. A_{43} Installation of a public lighting management system. A_{44} Study of the municipal lighting.	Not applicable
S_5 - Industry	Not applicable	I_{51} Interventions by the relevant companies, including among others, replacement of boilers or installation of CHP for heating. I_{52} Ventilation with heat recovery. I_{53} Solar cooling for industrial processes. I_{54} BEMS.

continued on next page

Table 2. Continued

Sector	Actions by the Local Authorities	Interventions by the Local Population
S_6 - **Municipal Fleet and Public Transport**	A_{61} Eco-driving seminars for the drivers of the municipal fleet. A_{62} Replacement of the municipal vehicles with new, more efficient vehicles. A_{63} Converting diesel municipal vehicles to LPG. A_{64} Efficient management of the municipal fleet. A_{65} Municipal fleet maintenance.	Not applicable
S_7 - **Private and Commercial Transport**	A_{71} Eco-driving promotion in the private transportation. A_{72} Information events on the new vehicle technologies. A_{73} Cycle paths. A_{74} Traffic study. A_{75} Increase the use of public transport and alternative modes of transport. A_{76} Use of biofuels.	I_{71} Adoption of the eco-driving. I_{72} Use of LPG, hybrid, new technology vehicles. I_{73} Use of bikes and public transportation. I_{74} Use of the "car sharing" or "car pooling" concept.
S_8 - **Local electricity production**	A_{81} Installation of photovoltaic in the municipal buildings. A_{82} Installation of lighting points with photovoltaic panel. A_{83} Promotion of the installation of small PV parks in agricultural lands.	I_{81} Photovoltaics. I_{82} Wind farms. I_{83} Small dams and hydroelectric power plants. I_{84} Power plants using biomass. I_{85} CHP unites using natural gas.
S_9 - **Local District Heating / Cooling**	A_{91} CHP units using natural gas. A_{92} Heating / cooling production unit using biomass. A_{93} Development / enhancement of district heating network.	Not applicable

series of questionnaires interspersed with controlled opinion feedback (Adler and Ziglio, 1996). Delphi represents a useful communication device among a group of experts and thus facilitates the formation of a group judgement (Helmer, 1977). According to Fowles study anonymity, controlled feedback, and statistical response characterize Delphi (Fowles, 1978). Delphi Method has been applied to a number of problems, such as primary-energy sources and socio-economic development (de Oliveira Matias and Devezas, 2007) and small-sized biogas systems (Cheng et al., 2014).

More specifically, the adopted approach includes the following steps:

Step 1: Experts' Identification – Identification of a number of key experts, mainly from Austria, Bulgaria, Germany, Greece and Portugal, including the following categories: "Energy agencies, utilities and energy companies", "Planners, developers" and "National, regional, municipal institutions".

Figure 4. Range of application for each alternative scenario

Scenario	Agriculture	Municipal Sector	Residential Sector	Tertiary Sector	Public Lighting	Transport	Local Electricity Production	Local Heat/Cold Production
1	12%	50%	10%	10%	50%	12%	100%	100%
2	5%	20%	4%	4%	20%	5%	100%	100%
3	5%	5%	4%	4%	5%	5%	100%	100%
4	10%	5%	5%	5%	5%	10%	100%	100%
5	12%	50%	10%	10%	50%	12%	75%	100%
6	5%	20%	4%	4%	20%	5%	75%	100%
7	5%	5%	4%	4%	5%	5%	75%	100%
8	10%	5%	5%	5%	5%	10%	75%	100%
9	12%	50%	10%	10%	50%	12%	75%	75%
10	5%	20%	4%	4%	20%	5%	75%	75%
11	5%	5%	4%	4%	5%	5%	75%	75%
12	10%	5%	5%	5%	5%	10%	75%	75%
13	12%	50%	10%	10%	50%	12%	50%	75%
14	5%	20%	4%	4%	20%	5%	50%	75%
15	5%	5%	4%	4%	5%	5%	50%	75%
16	10%	5%	5%	5%	5%	10%	50%	75%
17	12%	50%	10%	10%	50%	12%	100%	0%
18	5%	20%	4%	4%	20%	5%	100%	0%
19	5%	5%	4%	4%	5%	5%	100%50%	0%
20	10%	5%	5%	5%	5%	10%	100%	0%
21	12%	50%	10%	10%	50%	12%	75%	0%
22	5%	20%	4%	4%	20%	5%	75%	0%
23	5%	5%	4%	4%	5%	5%	75%	0%
24	10%	5%	5%	5%	5%	10%	75%	0%
25	12%	50%	10%	10%	50%	12%	50%	0%
26	5%	20%	4%	4%	20%	5%	50%	0%
27	5%	5%	4%	4%	5%	5%	50%	0%
28	10%	5%	5%	5%	5%	10%	50%	0%
29	12%	50%	10%	10%	50%	12%	0%	0%
30	5%	20%	4%	4%	20%	5%	0%	0%
31	5%	5%	4%	4%	5%	5%	0%	0%
32	10%	5%	5%	5%	5%	10%	0%	0%

Step 2: Questionnaires for the Key Parameters' Selection – The identified experts were asked to evaluate key parameters of each sector (municipal, tertiary, residential, transport, agriculture/forestry/fishery and industry sector). A number of questions was developed. Each question could be answered with only one of the following ways: objective multiple choice marking the desired option with an "x", alternatives' rating based on Likert scale from 1 to 5 (the value of 1 is assigned to the lowest importance/impact and value of 1 is assigned to the highest importance/impact).

Step 3: Questionnaires' Distribution & Analysis – Distribution of the questionnaires to the experts with various methods, such as through email, direct interviews with selected experts, etc. Data gathered from the questionnaires were processed (e.g. use of SPSS Statistics, a software package used for statistical analysis) through the calculation of the descriptive statistics (e.g. averages, standard deviations etc).

Step 4: Development of the Proposed Model – The overall algorithm for the future scenarios was developed.

Step 5: Comments and Feedback from Experts on the Proposed Model – The key experts were asked to comment and provide feedback on the proposed model, generating new ideas and solutions. The responses are compiled and analyzed.

In depth analysis of the key stakeholders in each country was carried out and for each country a number of different experts were identified. A total of 210 experts (national, regional, municipal institutions; energy agencies, utilities and energy companies; planners, developers) were identified. The experts were asked to provide their preferences and options for a number of parameters, such as:

- Rate of population growth at national level by 2020;
- Rate of electricity and fuels prices by 2020;
- Rate of energy consumption growth by 2020 of the tertiary, residential, industry, transport and agriculture sector;
- Rate of per capita gross domestic product by 2020;
- Annual heating and cooling degree days.

The contribution of the key parameters to each sector (tertiary, residential, transport, agriculture/forestry/fishery and industry sector) is described below (Table 3):

Table 3. Contribution of each parameter to the estimated energy consumption

	Tertiary	Residential	Industry	Transport	Agriculture/ Forestry/Fishery
Rate of population growth at municipal level	20%	35%	-	35%	30%
Rate of per capita gross domestic product at municipal level	35%	25%	-	15%	-
Annual heating and cooling degree days at municipal level	10%	10%	-	-	-
Rate of electricity and fuel prices	10%	10%	40%	20%	20%
Rate of energy consumption growth of the relevant sector at national level	25%	20%	60%	25%	50%
Development of the road network	-	-	-	5%	-

- **Municipal Buildings, Equipment/Facilities:** The estimated energy consumption of the municipal buildings, equipment and facilities is related to the aggregation of the energy consumption of each category (schools, municipal buildings and equipment/facilities), taking also into consideration the following parameters:
  - **Schools:** Rate of population growth (age 0-19) at municipal level;
  - **Municipal Buildings:** Stable energy consumption;
  - **Equipment/Facilities:** Rate of population growth at municipal level.
- **Tertiary or Residential Sector:** The estimated energy consumption of the tertiary or residential sector is related to the relevant energy consumption in the baseline year, in combination with a number of local parameters and the rate of energy consumption growth at national level adjusted to the municipal level, as follows:
  - Rate of population growth at municipal level;
  - Rate of per capita gross domestic product growth at municipal level, taking also into consideration a correction factor;
  - Annual heating and cooling degree days at municipal level multiplied by the rate of per capita gross domestic product growth at municipal level and divided by the heating and cooling degree days at national level, respectively;

- ◦ Rate of electricity and fuels prices, taking also into consideration a correction factor;
- ◦ Rate of energy consumption growth by 2020 of the tertiary sector at national level adjusted to the municipal level, according to the following parameters.
- ◦ Per capita gross domestic product at municipal level divided by per capita gross domestic product at national level;
- ◦ Annual heating degree days at municipal level divided by annual heating degree days at national level, taking also into consideration the rate of per capita gross domestic product growth at municipal level;
- ◦ Annual heating degree days at municipal level divided by annual heating degree days at national level, taking also into consideration the rate of per capita gross domestic product growth at municipal level.

It should be noted that the impact of the population growth is considered higher in the residential sector compared to the tertiary sector. On the other hand, the per capita gross domestic product growth will contribute significantly in the estimated energy consumption of the tertiary sector. Moreover, the annual heating degree days have increased impact on the estimated energy consumption for heating (heating oil, natural gas, etc), while the annual cooling degree days contribute significantly to the estimated electricity consumption.

- **Public Lighting:** The rate of population growth at municipal level is the key parameter.
- **Industries:** The estimated energy consumption of the industry sector is related to the energy consumption in the baseline year, in combination with the rate of electricity and fuels prices and the rate of energy consumption growth by 2020 of the industry sector at national level.
- **Municipal Fleet or Public Transport:** The estimated energy consumption of the municipal fleet is considered stable.
- **Private and Commercial Transport:** Similar to the tertiary or residential sector, the estimated energy consumption of the transport sector is related to a number of local parameters and the rate of energy consumption growth at national level, as follows:
- ◦ Rate of population growth at municipal level;
- ◦ Rate of per capita gross domestic product growth at municipal level, taking also into consideration a correction factor;

o   Rate of fuels prices, taking also into consideration a correction factor;

o   Rate of energy consumption growth by 2020 of the transport sector at national level, adjusted to the municipal level according to the per capita gross domestic product at municipal level divided by per capita gross domestic product at national level and a correction factor;

o   Development of the road network.

- **Agriculture/Forestry/Fishery:** The rates of population growth at municipal level, electricity and fuels prices, as well as energy consumption growth by 2020 of the agricultural sector are the key parameters, taking also into consideration the relevant correction factors.

Following the identification of key parameters, the overall algorithm for the future estimated progress of the consumptions and CO_2 reductions was developed (Marinakis et al., 2016).

Municipal Buildings, Equipment/Facilities

$$ECM_{es-e} = EC_{Ms-e} \times \left(1 + PG_{0-19}\right) + EC_{Mb-e} + EC_{Mef-e} \times \left(1 + PG\right) \qquad (1)$$

$$EC_{Mes-h} = EC_{Ms-h} \times \left(1 + PG_{0-19}\right) + EC_{Mb-h} \qquad (2)$$

$$EC_{Mes-ng} = EC_{Ms-ng} \times \left(1 + PG_{0-19}\right) + EC_{Mb-ng} + EC_{Mef-ng} \times \left(1 + PG\right) \qquad (3)$$

$$EC_{Mes-b} = EC_{Ms-b} \times \left(1 + PG_{0-19}\right) + EC_{Mb-b} \qquad (4)$$

$$EC_{Mes-d} = EC_{Mef-d} \times \left(1 + PG\right) \qquad (5)$$

Tertiary Sector

$$EC_{Tes-e} = 0.2 \times EC_{T-e} \times (1 + PG) + 0.35 \times EC_{T-e} \times (1 + GDP_{pcM} \times a) + 0.1 \times EC_{T-e} \times$$

$$\left[1 + \left(0.15 \times GDP_{pc\,M} \times HDD_M / HDD_N + 0.85 \times GDP_{pcM} \times CDD_M / CDD_N\right)\right] +$$

$$0.1 \times EC_{T-e} \times \left(1 - P_e \times b\right) + 0.25 \times EC_{T-e} \times [1 + ECG_T \times (1 + 0.5 \times GDP_{pcM/N} +$$

$$0.1 \times GDP_{pcM} \times HDD_{M/N} + 0.4 \times GDP_{pcM} \times CDD_{M/N}) \times c] \qquad (6)$$

$$EC_{Tes-h} = 0.2 \times EC_{T-h} \times \left(1 + PG\right) + 0.35 \times EC_{T-h} \times \left(1 + GDP_{pcM} \times a\right) + 0.10 \times EC_{T-h} \times$$

$$\left[1 + (0{,}9 \times GDP_{pcM} \times HDD_M + 0{,}1 \times GDP_{pcM} \times CDD_M) / HDD_N\right] + 0.1 \times EC_{T-h} \times (1 - P_f \times b)$$

$$+0.25 \times EC_{T-h} \times$$
$$\left[1 + ECG_T \times \left(0.5 \times GDP_{pcM/N} + 0.45 \times HDD_{M/N} + 0.05 \times CDD_{M/N}\right) \times c\right]$$
$$(7)$$

$$EC_{Tes-b} = 0.2 \times EC_{T-b} \times (1 + PG) + 0.35 \times EC_{T-b} \times (1 + GDP_{pcM} \times a) + 0.10 \times EC_{T-b} \times$$

$$\left[1 + (0{,}9 \times GDP_{pcM} \times HDD_M + 0{,}1 \times GDP_{pcM} \times CDD_M) / HDD_N\right] +$$
$$0.1 \times EC_{T-b} \times (1 \quad P_b \times b)$$
$$+0.25 \times EC_{T-b} \times$$
$$\left[1 + ECG_T \times \left(0.5 \times GDP_{pcM/N} + 0.45 \times HDD_{M/N} + 0.05 \times CDD_{M/N}\right) \times c\right]$$
$$(8)$$

$$EC_{Tes-ng} = 0.2 \times EC_{T-ng} \times (1 + PG) + 0.35 \times EC_{T-ng} \times (1 + GDP_{pcM} \times a) + 0.10 \times EC_{T-\,ng} \times$$

$$\left[1 + \left(0,9 \times GDP_{pcM} \times HDD_M + 0,1 \times GDP_{pcM} \times CDD_M\right) / HDD_N\right] +$$
$$0.1 \times EC_{T-ng} \times \left(1 - P_{ng} \times b\right)$$
$$+0.25 \times EC_{T-ng} \times$$
$$\left[1 + ECG_T \times \left(0.5 \times GDP_{pcM/N} + 0.45 \times HDD_{M/N} + 0.05 \times CDD_{M/N}\right) \times c\right]$$

$$(9)$$

Residential Sector

$$EC_{Res-e} = 0.35 \times EC_{R-e} \times \left(1 + PG\right) + 0.25 \times EC_{R-e} \times \left(1 + GDP_{pcM} \times a\right) + 0.1 \times EC_{R-e} \times$$

$$\left[1 + \left(0.15 \times GDP_{pcM} \times HDD_M / HDD_N + 0.85 \times GDP_{pcM} \times CDD_M / CDD_N\right)\right] + 0.1 \times EC_{R-e} \times$$

$$\left(1 - P_e \times b\right) + 0.2 \times EC_{R-e} \times[1 + ECG_R \times(1 + 0.5 \times GDP_{pcM/N} + 0.1 \times GDP_{pcM} \times HDD_{M/N}$$

$$+ 0.4 \times GDP_{pcM} \times CDD_{M/N}) \times c]$$

$$(10)$$

$$EC_{Res-h} = 0.35 \times EC_{R-h} \times \left(1 + PG\right) + 0.25 \times EC_{R-h} \times$$
$$\left(1 + GDP_{pcM} \times a\right) + 0.1 \times EC_{R-h} \times[1$$

$$+ \left(0,9 \times GDP_{pcM} \times HDD_M + 0,1 \times GDP_{pcM} \times CDD_M\right) / HDD_N]$$

$$+0.1 \times EC_{R-h} \times \left(1 - P_f \times b\right) +$$

$$0.2 \times EC_{R-h} \times$$
$$\left[1 + ECG_R \times \left(0.5 \times GDP_{pcM/N} + 0.45 \times HDD_{M/N} + 0.05 \times CDD_{M/N}\right) \times c\right]$$

$$(11)$$

$$EC_{Res-b} = 0.35 \times EC_{R-b} \times \left(1 + PG\right) + 0.25 \times EC_{R-b} \times$$
$$\left(1 + GDP_{pcM} \times a\right) + 0.1 \times EC_{R-b} \times$$

$$\left[1 + \left(0,9 \times GDP_{pcM} \times HDD_M + 0,1 \times GDP_{pcM} \times CDD_M \right) / HDD_N \right] +$$
$$0.1 \times EC_{R-b} \times \left(1 - P_b \times b \right) +$$
$$0.2 \times EC_{R-b} \times$$
$$\left[1 + ECG_R \times \left(0.5 \times GDP_{pcM/N} + 0.45 \times HDD_{M/N} + 0.05 \times CDD_{M/N} \right) \times c \right]$$

(12)

$$EC_{Res-ng} = 0.35 \times EC_{R-ng} \times \left(1 + PG \right) + 0.25 \times EC_{R-ng} \times \left(1 + GDP_{pcM} \times a \right)$$

$$+0.1 \times EC_{Rng} \times \left[1 + \left(0,9 \times GDP_{pcM} \times HDD_M + 0,1 \times GDP_{pcM} \times CDD_M \right) HDD_N \right]$$

$$+0.1 \times EC_{Rng} \times \left(1 - P_{ng} \times b \right) + 0.2 \times EC_{Rng} \times$$

$$\left[1 + ECG_T \times \left(0.5 \times GDP_{pcM/N} + 0.45 \times HDD_{M/N} + 0.05 \times CDD_{M/N} \right) \times c \right]$$

(13)

Public Lighting

$$EC_{PLes-e} = EC_{PL-e} \times \left(1 + PG \right)$$

(14)

Industries

$$EC_{Ies-e/h/d/ng/g} = 0.6 \times EC_{I-e/h/d/ng/g} \times \left(1 + ECG_{I \times a} \right) +$$
$$0.4 \times ECI \times \left(1 + P_{e/h/d/ng} \times b \right)$$

(15)

Municipal Fleet or Public Transport

$$EC_{MLPTes-d/g/ng/lg} = EC_{MLPT-d/g/ng/lg} \times \left(1 + PG \right)$$

(16)

Private and Commercial Transport

$$EC_{PCTes-d/g/ng/lg}$$

$$= 0.35 \times EC_{PCT-d/g/ng/lg} \times (1 + PG) + 0.15 \times EC_{PCT-d/g/ng/lg} \times (1 + GDP_{pcM \times a})$$

$$+ 0.2 \times EC_{PCT-d/g/ng/lg} \times \left(1 - P_{d/ng \times b}\right) + 0.25 \times EC_{PCT-d/g/ng/lg} \times [1$$

$$+ ECG_{PCT} \times (1 + GDP_{pcM/N}) \times c] + 0.05 \times EC_{PCT-d/g/ng/lg} \times (1 + 0.01 \times DV_{rn})$$

$$(17)$$

Agricultural Sector

$$EC_{Aes-e/d/g/ng} = 0.3 \times EC_{A-e/d/g/ng} \times \left(1 + PG\right) + 0.2 \times EC_{A-e/d/g/ng} \times \left(1 - P_{.\ x\ a}\right) + 0.5 \times EC_{A-e/d/g/ng} \times \left(1 + ECG_{A \times b}\right)$$

$$(18)$$

where:

- $EC_{Mpr-e/h/ng/b/d}$: Estimated electricity / heating oil / natural gas / biomass / diesel consumption in the municipal buildings, equipment/ facilities.
- $EC_{Tpr-e/h/b/ng}$: Estimated electricity / heating oil / biomass / natural gas / consumption in the tertiary sector.
- $EC_{Rpr-e/h/b/ng}$: Estimated electricity / heating oil / biomass / natural gas / consumption in the residential sector.
- EC_{PLpr-e}: Estimated electricity consumption in the public lighting.
- $EC_{Ipr-e/h/d/ng/g}$: Estimated electricity / heating oil / natural gas / gasoline consumption in the industrial sector.

- $EC_{MLPTpr-d/g/ng/lg}$: Estimated diesel / gasoline / natural gas / liquid gas consumption in the municipal fleet or public transport.
- $EC_{PCTpr-d/g/ng/lg}$: Estimated diesel / gasoline / natural gas / liquid gas consumption in the private and commercial transport.
- $EC_{Apr-e/d/g/ng}$: Estimated electricity / diesel / gasoline / natural gas consumption in the agricultural sector.
  - ○ $EC_{Ms-e/h/ng/b}$: Current electricity / heating oil / natural gas / biomass consumption in schools.
  - ○ $EC_{Mb-e/h/ng/b}$: Current electricity / heating oil / natural gas / biomass consumption in municipal buildings.
  - ○ $EC_{Mef-e/d/ng}$: Current electricity / diesel / natural gas consumption in equipment/facilities.
  - ○ $EC_{T-e/h/b/ng}$: Current electricity / heating oil / natural gas / consumption of the tertiary sector.
  - ○ $EC_{R-e/h/b/ng}$: Current electricity / heating oil / natural gas / consumption of the residential sector
  - ○ EC_{PL-e} : Current electricity consumption in the public lighting.
  - ○ $EC_{I-e/h/d/ng/g}$: Current electricity / heating oil / natural gas / gasoline consumption in the industrial sector.
  - ○ $EC_{MLPT-d/g/ng/lg}$: Current diesel / gasoline / natural gas / liquid gas consumption in the municipal fleet or public transport.
  - ○ EC_{PCT} : Current diesel / gasoline / natural gas / liquid gas consumption in the private and commercial transport.
  - ○ $EC_{A-e/d/g/ng}$: Current electricity / diesel / gasoline / natural gas consumption in the agricultural sector.
  - ○ PG: Rate of population growth at municipal level.
  - ○ PG_{0-19} : Rate of population growth (0-19 years old) at municipal level.
  - ○ $P_{e/h/d/ng}$: Rate of electricity / diesel / natural gas price.
  - ○ HDD_M : Annual heating degree days at municipal level.
  - ○ CDD_M : Annual cooling degree days at municipal level.
  - ○ HDD_N : Average value of annual heating degree days at national level.

○ CDD_N : Average value of annual cooling degree days at national level.

○ $HDD_{M/N}$: Annual heating degree days at municipal level / Average value of annual heating degree days at national level.

○ $CDD_{M/N}$: Annual cooling degree days at municipal level / Average value of annual cooling degree days at national level.

○ GDP_{pcM} : Rate of per capita gross domestic product at municipal level.

○ $GDP_{pcM/N}$: Per capita gross domestic product at municipal level / Per capita gross domestic product at national level.

○ ECG_{pct} : Rate of energy consumption growth of the transport sector at national level.

○ $ECG_{T/R/I/PCT/A}$: Rate of energy consumption growth of the tertiary/residential/industry/private and commercial transport/ agricultural sector at national level.

○ DV_{rn} : Development index of road network.

○ a, b, c: Correction factors (different in each sector).

Stakeholders' Engagement

Stakeholders' engagement in the decision-making process of the Action Plan's elaboration and development is crucial. To this end, a participatory planning approach can be used, in order to have a first evaluation of the alternative scenarios. A mix of qualitative and quantitative techniques are proposed in this step to approach stakeholders, including emailing, phone interviews, face-to-face meetings, questionnaires, focus groups, consultation meetings, workshops.

Aspiration Level

Following the development of alternative scenarios and the participatory planning, all the proposed scenarios are evaluated, initially, through aspiration levels. The approach involves the decision-maker choosing level of the objective that he desires to achieve regarding CO_2 emissions reduction (aspiration level).

"CHOOSE" COMPONENT

Criteria Selection

A number of criteria have been identified, according to the needs and opportunities of the sustainable development dimensions, namely the economic, social and environmental (Marinakis et al., 2017). The selection of criteria is based on the proposed indicators by the Covenant that could be used by the local authority to describe key actions highlighted as Benchmarks of Excellence. Most of these criteria have been also applied to solve multicriteria problems in other related energy aspects, such as the formulation of sustainable technological energy priorities (Doukas et al., 2010; 2007), identification of sustainable energy technology priorities for electricity generation under Clean Development Mechanism (Karakosta et al., 2009), ranking of renewable energy supply systems (Şengül et al., 2015) and evaluation of thermal-energy storage (Cavallaro, 2010).

The selected criteria satisfy the following requirements: monotony; exhaustiveness; cohesiveness; and non redundancy (Roy, 1985). Under these requirements we ensure consistency of the family. Moreover, the selected criteria are preferentially independent, namely the trade-offs between the g_i and g_j criteria are not dependent on the values of the rest of the criteria (Siskos et al., 2014).

More specifically, the necessary hypothesis to validate an additive value function for a given decision maker is the preferential independence of all criteria.

The identified criteria are the following (Figure 5):

- *g_1 – Investment Cost for the Municipality (Quantitative Criterion - €):* Economic magnitude, expressing the cost for the implementation of renewable energy and rational use of energy actions by the local authorities. The cost may include actions in the municipal buildings, equipment/facilities, public lighting, municipal fleet and public transport, local energy production, as well as awareness raising activities in the agricultural, residential, tertiary sector and transport. The estimated investment cost for the municipality can be calculated by the following equation:

$$IC = \sum_{i=1}^{m}\sum_{k=1}^{l} IC_{A_{ik}} \qquad (19)$$

where $IC_{A_{ik}}$ the investment due to the implementation of the action A_{ik} by the local authorities; i represent the number of sector and k the number of action within the relevant sector (S_1 - Agricultural/ Fishery/ Forestry Sector; S_2 - Municipal Buildings, Equipment/ Facilities; S_3 - Residential & Tertiary Sector; S_4 - Public Lighting; S_5 – Industry; S_6 - Municipal Fleet and Public Transport; S_7 - Private and Commercial Transport; S_8 - Local electricity production and S_9 - Local District Heating / Cooling). All the actions A_{ik} are presented in Table 2. The higher the cost of the examined Scenario, the lower is its performance to this criterion.

- g_2 – *Weighted Average Cost of Energy Saving (Quantitative Criterion - €/kWh):* Evaluation of the potential profitability of the examined Scenario through the following equation.

$$\begin{pmatrix} \text{Weighted} \\ \text{Average} \\ \text{Cost of} \\ \text{Energy Saving} \end{pmatrix} = \frac{\begin{pmatrix} \text{Initial Investment} \\ \text{Cost} \end{pmatrix} \times \dfrac{ir}{1-\left(ir+1\right)^{-Duration}} + \begin{pmatrix} \text{Annual Maintenance} \\ \text{Cost} \end{pmatrix}}{\text{Annual Energy Saving}}$$

$$(20)$$

Figure 5. The multicriteria evaluation system

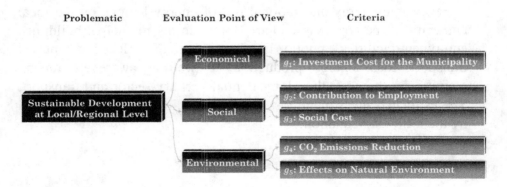

where ir is the interest rate.

It should be note that this criterion integrates the present value of the Scenarios' cash flow, ensuring in this way the independence property among criteria. It was selected since represents the minimum rate of return at which the authority produces value for its investors. The higher the value of the examined Scenario, the lower is its performance to this criterion.

- g_3 – *Contribution to Employment (Qualitative Criterion):* Reflects the impact of the examined Scenario in the social dimension regarding the creation of new jobs. The employment generated is often divided into two categories: investment (the most employment intensive part) and operation / maintenance (which last for the entire project's lifetime). It is a qualitative criterion and is derived as average value of the proposed actions in each Scenario. The performance of this criterion is assigned based on a 1-5 ordered qualitative scale, namely "1" very low (lower than 1%[1]), "2" low (higher than 1% and lower than 2%[2]), "3" moderate (higher than 2% and lower than 3%[2]), "4" high (higher than 3% and lower than 4%[2]) and "5" very high (higher than 4%[2]) contribution to employment regarding the particular Scenario.
- g_4 – *Social Cost (Quantitative Criterion - €/resident):* Reflects the total investment cost from the interventions of the local population (agricultural and residential sector, transport, etc). The estimated social cost can be calculated by the following equation:

$$IC = \sum_{i=1}^{m}\sum_{k=1}^{l}IC_{I_{ik}} \tag{21}$$

where $IC_{I_{ik}}$ the social cost due to the implementation of the intervention I_{ik} by the local population. i represent the number of sector and k the number of action within the relevant sector. All the actions I_{ik} are presented in Table 2. The higher the social cost of the examined Scenario, the lower is its performance to this criterion.

- g_5 – *CO_2 Emissions Reduction (Quantitative Criterion - %):* Estimated reduction of the CO_2 emissions that will be achieved through the implementation of all the proposed renewable energy and rational use of energy actions of each Scenario by 2020. The calculation of this criterion is based on the following data:

- ◦ Development of the baseline *emission* inventory;
- ◦ Estimation of the total CO_2 emissions reduction by 2020 using the calculations for the energy saving and production and related emissions factors.

$$CO2_{\%} = \frac{CO2_{base} - CO2_{reduction}}{CO2_{base}}$$

$$CO2_{base} = \sum_{i=1}^{m} \sum_{j=1}^{n} EC_{S_i j} \; x \, EF_j$$

$$CO2_{reduction} = \sum_{i=1}^{m} \sum_{j=1}^{n} \left(\sum_{k=1}^{l} ER_{A_{ik} j} \; x \, EF_i + \sum_{k=1}^{l} ER_{I_{ik} j} \; x \, EF_i \right) \tag{22}$$

where:

$CO2_{\%}$: Percentage of CO_2 emissions reduction due to the implementation of the Scenario (%)

$CO2_{base}$: Total CO_2 emissions in the baseline year ($tnCO_2$)

$CO2_{reduction}$: Total CO_2 emissions reduction due to the implementation of the Scenario ($tnCO_2$)

$EC_{S_i j}$: Consumption of the type of energy j in the sector S_i (MWh); for j

= 1: electricity, 2: heat/cold, 3: natural gas, 4: liquid gas, 5: heating oil, 6: diesel, 7: gasoline, 8: biomass, 9: solar thermal, 10: electricity, 11: other.

EF_j : Emission factor for the type of energy j ($tnCO_2$/MWh).

$ER_{A_{ik} j}$, $ER_{I_{ik} j}$: Energy reduction of the type of energy j due to the energy saving/production of the action A_{ik} and / or the intervention I_{ik}.

The higher the emissions reductions of the examined Scenario, the higher is its performance to this criterion.

- g_6 – *Effects on Natural Environment (Qualitative Criterion):* Reflects the Scenarios' interference level regarding the natural environment (e.g. visual intrusion, pressure on land resources and excessive land use). The performance of this criterion is assigned based on a 1-5 ordered qualitative scale, namely "1" very high, "2" high, "3" moderate, "4" low and "5" very low impact regarding the particular Scenario.

Following the criteria descriptions, the relevant evaluation scales are depicted in Table 4.

Multicriteria Ordinal Regression Approach

An additive value model is proposed. A number of methods to obtain the proposed value system can be found in the literature (Figueira et al., 2005; Keeney, 1992; Farquhar, 1984), which requires explicit trade-offs between economic, political and social criteria. Taking into account the amount of cognitive effort needed, or for ethical reasons, their application in real world decision environments remains questionable. To this end, the analysts prefer to infer the additive value model from global preference structures, by applying disaggregation or ordinal regression methods. A survey of these methods and synergy of methods for the assessment of additive value models was recently presented by Hurson and Siskos (2014), such as MACBETH technique, the standard MAUT trade-off analysis and UTA-based methods (UTA I, UTA II, UTAGMS, GRIP, RUTA, etc.). UTA methods not only adopt the aggregation disaggregation principles, but they may also be considered as the main initiative and the most representative example of preference disaggregation theory (Siskos, 2005).

Table 4. Criteria evaluation scale

	Index	Worst Level	Best Level
G1	Quantitative (€)	120,000,000	0
G2	Quantitative (€/kWh)	0.2	0
G3	Qualitative	1	5
G4	Quantitative (€/ resident)	2,000	0
G5	Quantitative (%)	20	100
G6	Qualitative	1	5

The proposed additive value model is described by the following form:

$$u(\mathbf{g}) = \sum_{i=1}^{n} p_i u_i(g_i) \tag{23}$$

subject to normalization constraints:

$$\sum_{i=1}^{n} p_i = 1$$

$$u_i(g_{i_*}) = 0, \; u_i(g_i^*) = 1, \forall i = 1,2,\ldots,n \tag{24}$$

where $\mathbf{g} = (g_1, g_2, \ldots, g_n)$ is the performance vector of an alternative scenario on the n criteria; g_{i_*} and g_i^* are the least and most preferable levels of the criterion g_i, respectively; $u_i, i = 1,2,\ldots n$ are non-decreasing real valued functions, named marginal value or utility functions, which are normalized between 0 and 1, and p_i is the relative weight of u_i.

Both the marginal and the global value functions have the monotonicity property of the true criterion. For instance, in the case of the global value function the following properties hold:

$$u[\mathbf{g}(a)] > u[\mathbf{g}(b)] \; ifa \succ b(preference)$$

$$u[\mathbf{g}(a)] = u[\mathbf{g}(b)] \; ifa \sim b(indifference) \tag{25}$$

The existence of the preference model assumes the preferential independence of the criteria for the decision maker (Keeney and Raiffa, 1976), while other conditions for additivity have been proposed by Fishburn (1966, 1967). This assumption does not pose significant problems in a posteriori analyses such as disaggregation analyses.

A number of methods to obtain the proposed value system can be found in the literature (Figueira et al., 2005; Keeney, 1992; Farquhar, 1984), which requires explicit trade-offs between economic, political and social criteria.

Taking into account the amount of cognitive effort needed, or for ethical reasons, their application in real world decision environments remains questionable.

To this end, the analysts prefers to infer the additive value model from global preference structures, by applying disaggregation or ordinal regression methods. A survey of these methods and synergy of methods for the assessment of additive value models is recently presented by Hurson and Siskos (2014), such as MACBETH technique, the standard MAUT trade-off analysis and UTA-based methods (UTA I, UTA II, UTAGMS, GRIP, RUTA, etc).

Over the past three decades UTA-based methods have been applied in several real-world decision-making problems (see Siskos et al., 2005 for a comprehensive survey on UTA methods and applications), with the most recent efforts focused on e-government (Siskos et al., 2013; 2014). Although, UTA method has been applied to a number of problems regarding sustainable development, such as energy efficiency, wastewater treatment and environmental issues (Sola & Mota, 2012; Demesouka et al., 2013; Kholghi, 2001), there are not studies regarding sustainable energy planning at local / regional level.

In this context, a flexible and transparent approach is the UTA II method, proposed by Siskos J. (1980), which has been used for the examined decision aiding problem. This method aims at inferring one or more additive value functions from a given ranking on a reference set of actions A_R (Jacquet-Lagrèze and Siskos, 1982). It uses special linear programming techniques to assess these functions so that the ranking(s) obtained through these functions on A_R is as consistent as possible with the given one. UTA II method includes the following two phases:

- *Phase I: Construction of the marginal value functions $u_i\left(g_i\right)$*. The idea of least square approximation is used, in order to fit a polynomial function P(x) to a set of data points (x_i, y_i) having a number of theoretical solution (provided by the decision maker through an interactive process).

- *Phase II: Estimation of the criteria weights p_i*
  - Selection of a reference set: For the construction of the reference set by the analyst, virtual scenarios are selected. The decision maker is asked to provide a ranking (weak order) of the virtual scenarios. In each comparison, the two scenarios are differed in two or at most three criteria values, so as to be possible by the decision maker to evaluate the scenarios. As result, the scenarios

of the reference set $A_R = \{a_1, a_2, \ldots, a_m\}$ are rearranged in such a way that $a_i \succ a_{i+1}$ or $a_i \sim a_{i+1}$.

○ Linear programming techniques: UTA II introduces two error functions σ^+ and σ^- on A_R by writing for each pair of consecutive actions in the ranking the analytic expressions:

$$\triangle (a_i, a_{i+1}) = \sum_{i=1}^{n} p_i \{u_i [g_i (a_i)] - u_i [g_i (a_{i+1})]\} - \sigma^+ (a_i) + \sigma^- (a_i) + \sigma^+ (a_{i+1}) - \sigma^- (a_{i+1})$$

(26)

where:

$a_i \in A_R$ and $\sigma^+ (a_i), \sigma^- (a_i)$ are the overestimation and the underestimation error respectively.

Then, the following linear program is solved:

$$[min] F = \sum_{i=1}^{m} \sigma^+ (a_i) + \sigma^- (a_i)$$

subject to:

$$\Delta (a_i, a_{i+1}) \geq \delta, if\, a_i \succ a_{i=1}$$

$$\Delta (a_i, a_{i+1}) = 0, if\, a_i \sim a_{i=1}$$

$$\sum_{i=1}^{n} p_i = 1, \ p_i \geq 0, \sigma^+ (a_i) \geq 0, \sigma^- (a_i) \geq 0 \ \forall a_i \in A_R$$

with δ being a small positive number. (27)

Moreover, the existence of multiple or near optimal solutions of the above linear program is evaluated. To this end, the mean additive value function of near optimal solutions which maximize the functions $u_i \left(g_i^* \right)$ on the polyhedron of the constraints of the linear program (8) is calculated.

Robustness Analysis

Another important issue is the robustness of the evaluation model. UTA[GMS], GRIP, RUTA, extreme ranking analysis and the robustness measurement control are the most recent UTA-type methods (Greco et al., 2008; Figueira et al., 2009; Kadzinski et al., 2013; Kadzinski et al. (2012); Kadzinski & Tervonen, 2013a, 2013b; Greco et al., 2012). In this context, the adopted approach search for multiple solutions based on the use of the extreme ranking analysis of Kadzinski et al. (2012). The approach evaluates the performance of each alternative relative to all other alternatives in a reference set A, determining the best and the worst ranks, and the score that an alternative can attain.

In order to identify the highest rank of an alternative in the ranking provided by any compatible value function (or any compatible outranking mode) the following mixed integer linear program is calculated:

$$\left[min\right] F = \sum_{b \in A \setminus \{a\}} u_b$$

Subject to:

$$E_u^{A_R}$$

$$U\left(a\right) \geq U\left(b\right) - Mv_b$$

for all $b \in A \setminus \{a\}$ (28)

where M is an auxiliary variable equal to a big positive value and v_b is a new binary variable associated with comparison of a to alternative b. In order to identify the lowest rank of an alternative in the ranking provided by any compatible value function (or any compatible outranking mode) the following mixed integer linear program is calculated:

$$\left[min\right] F = \sum_{b \in A \setminus \{a\}} u_b$$

Subject to:

$$E_u^{A_R}$$

$$U\left(b\right) \geq U\left(a\right) + \varepsilon - Mv_b$$

for all $b \in A \setminus \left\{a\right\}$ (29)

where M is an auxiliary variable equal to a big positive value, ε is equal to a small positive value, and v_b is a new binary variable associated with comparison of a to alternative b.

"CHECK" COMPONENT

The final stage of the proposed framework includes the "Methodological Approach for Monitoring SEC Targets". The overall philosophy of the proposed approach is presented in Figure 6.

Indicators

The methodological approach consists of monitoring indicators that are structured in four main categories "Energy", "Environment", "Economy"," Infrastructure and ICT". Table 5 presents the indicators (I_{ij}) for each category "i".

The indicators are described more extensively in the following table.

The analysis descripted before, is summarized in the following Figure 7.

Description of the "SEC$_{Index}$"

The composite index "SEC$_{Index}$ (Sustainable Energy Community Index)" was introduced. The procedure for the development of the "SEC$_{Index}$" was based on a "proximity-to-target" approach. More specifically, for each indicator, the distance from the setting target is calculated. Thus, the values of the evaluation indicators are transformed into a scale of "0-100" with "100" to be the maximum efficiency and "0" the minimum efficiency.

Figure 6. Philosophy of the methodological approach for monitoring SEC targets

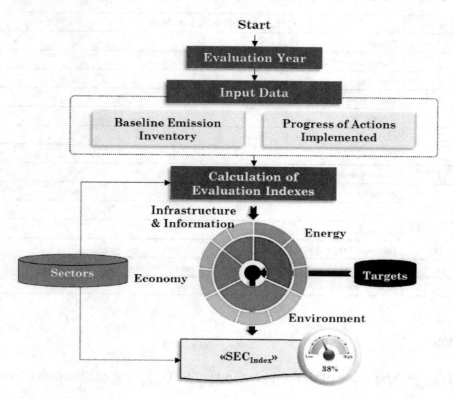

The "SEC$_{Index}$" is calculated based on a cumulative two-scale procedure. By taking as reference the ten evaluation indicators; the scores of the four categories are calculated, and thus the "SEC$_{Index}$" composite index. It is noted that each evaluation indicator is assessed in each category with a different weighting factor. The determination of the weighting factors is completed with the participation of experts, through filling in appropriate questionnaires (in parallel with the procedure that was followed for the equations of the future estimated progress of the consumptions and CO_2 reductions. The values of the weighting factors are shown in Table 7.

Based on the previous analysis, the equation for the calculation of the "SEC$_{Index}$" in each activity sector is the following:

$$SEC_{Index\_k} = \sum_{i=1}^{4} \sum_{j=1}^{2 \blacklozenge 3} w_{ij} \frac{I_{evaluation\_ij} - I_{base\_ij}}{I_{target\_ij} - I_{base\_ij}} \tag{30}$$

Table 5. Monitoring indicators

Symbol	Evaluation Indicators
I_1	**Energy**
I_{11}	Energy consumption per capita
I_{12}	Electricity use in final energy consumption
I_{13}	Use of fossil fuels in final energy consumption
I_2	**Environment**
I_{21}	CO_2 emissions per capita
I_{22}	CO_2 emission intensity
I_{23}	Use of renewable energy sources
I_3	**Economy**
I_{31}	Total budget spent
I_{32}	Actions funding through external sources
I_4	**Infrastructure and ICT**
I_{41}	Level of integration of automations, smart meters and ICT solutions
I_{42}	Level of awareness

where:

SEC_{Index_k} The value of the complex index "SEC_{Index}" for each activity sector k

w_{ij} The weighting factor of index j of category i

I_{target_ij} The target for evaluation index I_{ij}

I_{base_ij} The value of evaluation index I_{ij} for the base year

$I_{evaluation\_ij}$ The value of evaluation index I_{ij} for the evaluation year

Thus, the "SEC_{Index}" index shows the progress achieved in the specific activity sector in regards to the accomplishment of the targets which were defined during the development of the Sustainable Energy and Climate Action Plan (Figure 8).

Table 6. Description of the monitoring indicators

I_{11}: Energy Consumption Per Capita	
Description	It reflects the final consumption of energy in each sector of the municipality.
Calculation	It comes as a result of the sum of individual consumptions per type of energy, divided with the total population of the municipality during the year of evaluation.
Units	MWh/capita
I_{12}: Use of Electricity in the Final Energy Consumption	
Description	It expresses the percentage of electricity usage in the final energy consumption.
Calculation	It comes as a result of the electricity energy consumption, divided by the total energy consumption in the sector of interest.
Units	Percentage (%)
I_{13}: Use of Fossil Fuels in Final Energy Consumption	
Description	It reflects the percentage of fossil fuel (gasoline, heat oil, diesel, etc.) in final energy consumption.
Calculation	It comes as a result of the consumption of fossil fuels, divided by the total energy consumption in the specific sector.
Units	Percentage (%)
I_{21}: CO_2 Emissions Per Capita	
Description	It indicates the total CO_2 emission in the specific area
Calculation	It comes as a result of the sum of CO_2 emission per form of energy, divided by the total population of the municipality during the year of evaluation.
Units	$tnCO_2$/capita
I_{22}: CO_2 Emissions Intensity	
Description	It expresses the scale of CO_2 emission per unit of consumption.
Calculation	It comes as a result of the sum of CO_2 emission per energy form, divided by the total energy consumption.
Units	$tnCO_2$/MWh
I_{23}: Use of Renewable Energy Sources	
Description	It reflects the penetration of renewable energy sources in the area.
Calculation	It comes as a result of the total production of energy from renewable energy sources (for electricity and heat/cooling), divided by the total population of the area during the year of evaluation.
Units	MWh/capita
I_{31}: Total Budget Spent	
Description	It indicates the total budget that has been exploited for the implementation of the expected measures and actions in each sector of activation.
Calculation	It comes as a result of the total budget spent, divided with the total population of the year during the year of evaluation.
Units	€/capita

continued on next page

Finally, for better visualization of the final results, the following graph

Table 6. Continued

I₃₂: Actions Funding Through External Sources	
Description	It indicates the total amount of funding for action through external sources.
Calculation	It comes as a result of the total amount of funding, divided with the total population of the area during the year of evaluation.
Units	€/capita
I₄₁: Level of Integration of Automations, Smart Meters and ICT Solutions	
Description	It expresses the level of integration of Automations, Smart Meters and ICT Solutions, etc.
Calculation	It comes as a result of the total energy monitored by the smart meters, BEMS, ICT, divided with the total energy consumption.
Units	Percentage (%)
I₄₂: Level of Awareness	
Description	It reflects all the final users in each sector that have participated in actions of orientation and awareness.
Calculation	It comes as a result of the percentage of final users that have participated in actions of orientation and awareness.
Units	Percentage (%)

Figure 7. Monitoring indicators

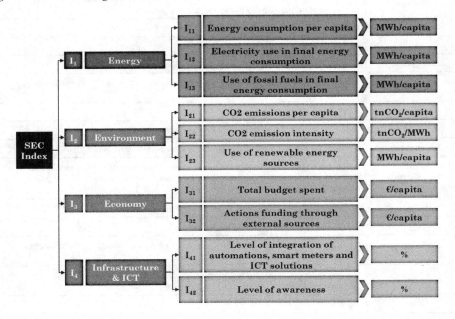

Table 7. Weights of the monitoring indicators

Category	Monitoring Indicator	Weight
Energy (32%)	Per capita energy consumption	12,8%
	Percentage of electricity use in final energy consumption	9,6%
	Percentage of fossil fuel use in final energy consumption	9,6%
Environment (35%)	Per capita CO_2 emissions	12,25%
	CO_2 emission intensity	10,85%
	Use of renewable energy sources	11,9%
Economy (19%)	Total budget spent	9,5%
	Percentage of funding from external sources	9,5%
Infrastructure & Information (14%)	Level of integration of automations, smart meters and ICT solutions	5,6%
	Level of awareness	8,4%

is used (Figure 9). It is noted that based on the values of "SEC_{Index}" of each activity sector, it is possible to calculate the total "SEC_{Index}" of the municipality.

CONCLUSION

The potential replication of the proposed framework relies on the necessity for the cities and communities to create their Sustainable Energy and Climate Action Plan. This stepwise framework, which guides the local and regional authorities in the development of the alternative Scenarios for the region and their evaluation, is simple, concise and comprehensive. The MPC$^+$ framework can be widely used by and support different types of municipalities. Moreover, its general formation is strictly based on the Guidelines provided by the Covenant of Mayors, while it has been enhanced with additional aspects, as summarized below:

- Integration of the mulricriteria analysis and robustness analysis in the Action Plan's development, providing a comprehensive evaluation of alternative Scenarios; support to the decision making for the selection of the most appropriate sustainable renewable energy and rational use of energy technologies for the Sustainable Energy and Climate Action Plan.

Figure 8. General philosophy of the "Methodological Framework for Approach SEC Targets"

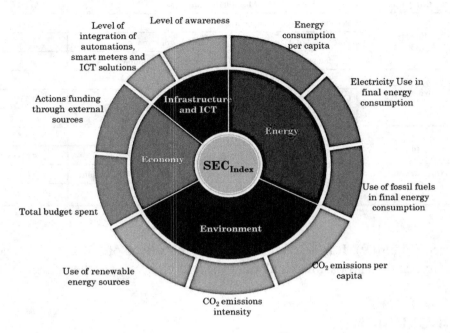

Figure 9. Visualization of the final results from the "SECIndex" index

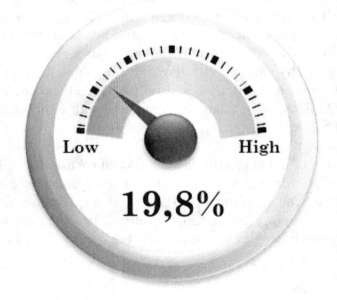

- A knowledge-based process for the initial design of alternative Scenarios in the region, taking into consideration its specific characteristics and main priorities (energy baseline, etc.).
- Integration of the local stakeholders' views on the formulation of alternative Scenarios for the region, raising the public awareness and making their citizens more self-conscious about the energy they consume and the new projects in the area.

ACKNOWLEDGMENT

A part of the current chapter was based on the relevant activities conducted within the framework of the project "Rural Web Energy Learning Network for Action – eReNet (Project no: IEE/10/224/SI2.593412), supported by the Intelligent Energy – Europe (IEE) Programme. The content of the chapter is the sole responsibility of its author and does not necessary reflect the views of the EC.

REFERENCES

Adler, M., & Ziglio, E. (1996). *Gazing into the oracle*. Bristol, PA: Jessica Kingsley Publishers.

Ardente, F., Beccali, G., Cellura, M., & Lo Brano, V. (2005). Life cycle assessment of a solar thermal collector. *Renewable Energy, 30*(7), 1031–1054. doi:10.1016/j.renene.2004.09.009

Babusiaux, D., & Pierru, A. (2007). Modelling and allocation of CO_2 emissions in a multiproduct industry: The case of oil refining. *Applied Energy, 84*(7-8), 828–841. doi:10.1016/j.apenergy.2007.01.013

Björklund, A., & Finnveden, G. (2003). *Recycling Revisited - Comparing Different Waste Management Strategies. 10th SETAC LCA Case Studies Symposium*, Barcelona, Spain.

Boehmer-Christiansen, S. (1994a). Global climate protection policy: The limits of scientific advice. *Part 1. Global Environ, 4*(2), 140–159. doi:10.1016/0959-3780(94)90049-3

Boehmer-Christiansen, S. (1994b). Global climate protection policy: The limits of scientific advice. *Part 2. Global Environ, 4*(2), 185–200. doi:10.1016/0959-3780(94)90002-7

Brown, L., Armstrong Brown, S., Jarvisa, S. C., Syedb, B., Goulding, K. W. T., Phillipsd, V. R., & Paina, B. F. et al. (2001). An inventory of nitrous oxide emissions from agriculture in the UK using the IPCC methodology: Emission estimate, uncertainty and sensitivity analysis. *Atmospheric Environment, 35*(8), 1439–1449. doi:10.1016/S1352-2310(00)00361-7

Cheng, S., Li, Z., Mang, H.-P., Neupane, K., Wauthelet, M., & Huba, E.-M. (2014). Application of fault tree approach for technical assessment of small-sized biogas systems in Nepal. *Applied Energy, 113,* 1372–1381. doi:10.1016/j.apenergy.2013.08.052

Cherubinia, F., Birda, N. D., Annette Cowieb, A., Jungmeiera, G., Schlamadingerc, B., & Woess-Gallascha, S. (2009). Energy- and greenhouse gas-based LCA of biofuel and bioenergy systems: Key issues, ranges and recommendations. *Resources, Conservation and Recycling, 53*(8), 434–447. doi:10.1016/j.resconrec.2009.03.013

CoM - Covenant of Mayors. (2017). *The Covenant of Mayors for Climate and Energy Reporting Guidelines*. Covenant of Mayors Office & Joint Research Centre of the European Commission. Retrieved January 21, 2017, from: http://www.covenantofmayors.eu/IMG/pdf/Covenant_ReportingGuidelines.pdf

de Oliveira Matias, J. C., & Devezas, T. C. (2007). Consumption Dynamics of Primary-Energy Sources: The Century of Alternative Energies. *Applied Energy, 84*(7-8), 763–770. doi:10.1016/j.apenergy.2007.01.007

Del Borghi, A., Binaghi, L., Del Borghi, M., & Gallo, M. (2005). *The Application of the Environmental Product Declaration to Waste Disposal in a Sanitary Landfill - Four Case Studies*. Environmental Product Declaration.

Demesouka, O.-E., Vavatsikos, A.-P., & Anagnostopoulos, K.-P. (2013). Spatial UTA (S-UTA) – A New Approach for Raster-Based GIS Multicriteria Suitability Analysis and its Use in Implementing Natural Systems for Wastewater Treatment. *Journal of Environmental Management, 125,* 41–54. doi:10.1016/j.jenvman.2013.03.035 PMID:23644589

Dones, R., Heck, T., & Hirschberg, S. (2004). Greenhouse Gas Emissions from Energy Systems, Comparison and Overview. Encyclopedia of Energy, 77-95.

Doukas, H., Botsikas, A., & Psarras, J. (2007). Multi-criteria decision aid for the formulation of sustainable technological energy priorities using linguistic variables. *European Journal of Operational Research*, *182*(2), 844–855. doi:10.1016/j.ejor.2006.08.037

Doukas, H., Karakosta, C., & Psarras, J. (2010). Computing with words to assess the sustainability of renewable energy options. *Expert Systems with Applications*, *37*(7), 5491–5497. doi:10.1016/j.eswa.2010.02.061

Emmenegger, M.F., Frischknecht, R, Stutz, M, Guggisberg, M, Witschi, R, & Otto, T. (2004). *Life Cycle Assessment of the Mobile Communication System UMTS: Toward Eco-Efficient Systems*. Academic Press.

Erlandsson, M., & Borg, M. (2003). Generic LCA-methodology applicable for buildings, constructions and operation services – today practice and development needs. *Building and Environment*, *38*(7), 919–938. doi:10.1016/S0360-1323(03)00031-3

Farquhar, P. H. (1984). Utility assessment methods. *Management Science*, *30*(11), 1283–1300. doi:10.1287/mnsc.30.11.1283

Figueira, J. R., Greco, S., & Słowinski, R. (2009). Building a Set of Additive Value Functions Representing a Reference Preorder and Intensities of Preference: GRIP Method. *European Journal of Operational Research*, *195*(2), 460–486. doi:10.1016/j.ejor.2008.02.006

Figueira, J., & Greco, S. (2005). Multiple Criteria Decision Analysis: State of the art Surveys. Dordrecht: Kluwer Academic Publishers.

Fishburn, P. (1966). A Note on Recent Developments in Additive Utility Theories for Multiple Factors Situations. *Operations Research*, *14*(6), 1143–1148. doi:10.1287/opre.14.6.1143

Fishburn, P. (1967). Methods for Estimating Additive Utilities. *Management Science*, *13*(7), 435–453. doi:10.1287/mnsc.13.7.435

Fowles, J. (1978). *Handbook of futures research*. Greenwood Press.

Góralczyk, M. (2003). Life-cycle assessment in the renewable energy sector. *Applied Energy*, *75*(3-4), 205–211. doi:10.1016/S0306-2619(03)00033-3

Greco, S., Mousseau, V., & Słowinski, R. (2008). Ordinal Regression Revisited: Multiple Criteria Ranking Using a set of Additive Value Functions. *European Journal of Operational Research*, *191*(2), 416–436. doi:10.1016/j.ejor.2007.08.013

Greco, S., Siskos, Y., & Słowinski, R. (2012). *Controlling Robustness in Ordinal Regression Models*. Paper presented at the 75th meeting of the EURO working group on MCDA, Tarragona, Spain.

Helmer, O. (1977). Problems in futures research: Delphi and causal cross-impact analysis. *Futures*, *9*(February), 17–31. doi:10.1016/0016-3287(77)90049-0

Hurson, C., & Siskos, Y. (2014). A Synergy of Multicriteria Techniques to Assess Additive Value Models. *European Journal of Operational Research*, *238*(2), 540–551. doi:10.1016/j.ejor.2014.03.047

IPCC. (2006). *2006 IPCC Guidelines for National Greenhouse Gas Inventories*. National Greenhouse Gas Inventories Programme. Retrieved July 11, 2016, from: http://www.ipcc-nggip.iges.or.jp/public/2006gl/ index.html

Jacquet-Lagrèze, E., & Siskos, Y. (1982). Assessing a Set of Additive Utility Functions for Multicriteria Decision Making: The UTA Method. *European Journal of Operational Research*, *10*(2), 151–164. doi:10.1016/0377-2217(82)90155-2

Kadzinski, M., Greco, S., & Slowinski, R. (2013). RUTA: A Framework for Assessing and Selecting Additive Value Functions on the basis of Rank Related Requirements. *Omega*, *41*(3), 735–751. doi:10.1016/j.omega.2012.10.002

Kadzinski, M., & Tervonen, T. (2013a). Stochastic Ordinal Regression for Multiple Criteria Sorting Problems. *Decision Support Systems*, *55*(1), 55–66. doi:10.1016/j.dss.2012.12.030

Kadzinski, M., & Tervonen, T. (2013b). Robust Multi-Criteria Ranking with Additive Value Models and Holistic Pair-Wise Preference Statements. *European Journal of Operational Research*, *228*(1), 169–180. doi:10.1016/j.ejor.2013.01.022

Kadzinski, M., Greco, S., & Slowinski, R. (2012). Extreme Ranking Analysis in Robust Ordinal Regression. *Omega*, *40*(4), 488–501. doi:10.1016/j.omega.2011.09.003

Karakosta, C., Doukas, H., & Psarras, J. (2009). Directing clean development mechanism towards developing countries sustainable development priorities. *Energy for Sustainable Development, 13*(2), 77–84. doi:10.1016/j.esd.2009.04.001

Keeney, R. L. (1992). *Value-focused thinking: a path to creative decision making*. London: Harvard UP.

Keeney, R. L., & Raiffa, H. (1976). *Decisions with Multiple Objectives: Preferences and Value Tradeoffs*. New York: John Wiley and Sons.

Khan, F. I., Hawboldt, K., & Iqbal, M. T. (2005). Life cycle analysis of wind fuel cell integrated system. *Renewable Energy, 30*(2), 157–177. doi:10.1016/j.renene.2004.05.009

Kholghi, M. (2001). Multi-Criterion Decision-Making Tools for Wastewater Planning Management. *Journal of Agricultural Science and Technology, 3*, 281–286.

La Motta, S., Santino, D., Ancona, P., & Weiss, W. (2005). CO_2 emission accounting for the non-energy use of fossil fuels in Italy: A comparison between NEAT model and the IPCC approaches. *Resources, Conservation and Recycling, 45*(3), 310–330. doi:10.1016/j.resconrec.2005.05.007

Lenzen, M., & Wachsmann, U. (2004). Wind turbines in Brazil and Germany: An example of geographical variability in life-cycle assessment. *Applied Energy, 77*(2), 119–130. doi:10.1016/S0306-2619(03)00105-3

Marinakis, V., Doukas, H., Xidonas, P., & Zopounidis, C. (2017). Multicriteria Decision Support in Local Energy Planning: An Evaluation of Alternative Scenarios for the Sustainable Energy Action Plan. *Omega – The International Journal of Management Science*.

Marinakis, V., Xidonas, P., & Doukas, H. (2016). A Modelling Framework for the Forecasting of Energy Consumption and CO_2 Emissions at Local/Regional Level. *International Journal of Global Energy Issues, 39*(6), 444–460. doi:10.1504/IJGEI.2016.079374

Martínez, E., Jiménez, E., Blanco, J., & Sanz, F. (2010). LCA sensitivity analysis of a multi-megawatt wind turbine. *Applied Energy, 87*(7), 2293–2303. doi:10.1016/j.apenergy.2009.11.025

Martínez, E., Sanz, F., Pellegrini, S., Jiménez, E., & Blanco, J. (2009). Life cycle assessment of a multi-megawatt wind turbine. *Renewable Energy, 34*(3), 667–673. doi:10.1016/j.renene.2008.05.020

Masruroh, N. A., Li, B., & Klemes, J. (2006). Life cycle analysis of a solar thermal system with thermochemical storage process. *Renewable Energy, 31*(4), 537–548. doi:10.1016/j.renene.2005.03.008

Nevison, C. (2000). Review of the IPCC methodology for estimating nitrous oxide emissions associated with agricultural leaching and runoff. *Chemosphere. Global Change Science, 2*(3-4), 493–500. doi:10.1016/S1465-9972(00)00013-1

O'Brien, D., Shalloo, L., Patton, J., Buckley, F., Grainger, C., & Wallace, M. (2012). Animal. Evaluation of the effect of accounting method, IPCC v. LCA, on grass-based and confinement dairy systems' greenhouse gas emissions. *Journal of Dairy Science, 6*(9), 1512–1527. PMID:23031525

Olivier Jos, G. J., & Peters Jeroen, A. H. W. (2005). CO_2 from non-energy use of fuels: A global, regional and national perspective based on the IPCC Tier 1 approach. *Resources, Conservation and Recycling, 45*(3), 210–225. doi:10.1016/j.resconrec.2005.05.008

Ortiz, O., Castells, F., & Sonnemann, G. (2009). Sustainability in the construction industry: A review of recent developments based on LCA. *Construction & Building Materials, 23*(1), 28–29. doi:10.1016/j.conbuildmat.2007.11.012

Ozeler, U., Yetis, & Demirer, G.N. (2006). Life Cycle Assessment of Municipal Solid Waste Management Methods: Ankara Case Study. *Enviro, 32*(3), 405–411. PMID:16310852

Papageorgiou, A., Barton, J. R., & Karagiannidis, A. (2009). Assessment of the greenhouse effect impact of technologies used for energy recovery from municipal waste: A case for England. *Journal of Environmental Management, 90*(10), 2999–3012. doi:10.1016/j.jenvman.2009.04.012 PMID:19482412

Pehnt, M. (2006). Dynamic life cycle assessment (LCA) of renewable energy technologies. *Renewable Energy, 31*(1), 55–1. doi:10.1016/j.renene.2005.03.002

Poritosh, R., Daisuke, N., Takahiro, O., Qingyi, X., Hiroshi, O., & Nobutaka, N. (2009). A review of life cycle assessment (LCA) on some food products. *Journal of Food Engineering, 90*(1), 1–10. doi:10.1016/j.jfoodeng.2008.06.016

Roy, B. (1985). *Méthodologie Multicritère d'Aide à la Décision.* Paris: Economica.

Şengül, Ü., Eren, M., Eslamian Shiraz, S., Gezder, V., & Şengül, A. B. (2015). Fuzzy TOPSIS method for ranking renewable energy supply systems in Turkey. *Renewable Energy, 75*, 617–625. doi:10.1016/j.renene.2014.10.045

Siskos, E., Malafekas, M., Askounis, D., & Psarras, J. (2013). E-government Benchmarking in European Union: A Multicriteria Extreme Ranking Approach. *IFIP Advances in Information and Communication Technology, 399*, 338–348. doi:10.1007/978-3-642-37437-1_28

Siskos, E., & Tsotsolas, N. (2015). Elicitation of Criteria Importance Weights through the Simos Method: A Robustness Concern. *European Journal of Operational Research, 246*(2), 543–553. doi:10.1016/j.ejor.2015.04.037

Siskos, J. (1980). Comment modéliser les preferences au moyen de fonctions dutilité additives. *RAIRO Recherche Opérationnelle, 14*(1), 53–82. doi:10.1051/ro/1980140100531

Siskos, Y., Grigoroudis, E., & Matsatsinis, N. (2005). The UTA methods. In J. Figueira, S. Greco, & M. Ehrgott (Eds.), Multiple criteria decision analysis: State of the art surveys (pp. 297–343). Dordrecht: Kluwer Academic Publishers. doi:10.1007/0-387-23081-5_8

Siskos, E., Askounis, D., & Psarras, J. (2014). Multicriteria Decision Support for Global e-Government Evaluation. *Omega, 46*, 51–63. doi:10.1016/j.omega.2014.02.001

Siskos, Y. (2001). Preference Disaggregation. Encyclopedia of Optimization, 2003-2014. doi:10.1007/0-306-48332-7_394

Sobrino, H. F., Rodríguez Monroya, C., & Hernández Pérez, J. L. (2011). Biofuels and fossil fuels: Life Cycle Analysis (LCA) optimisation through productive resources maximization. *Renewable & Sustainable Energy Reviews, 15*(6), 2621–2628. doi:10.1016/j.rser.2011.03.010

Sola, A.-V.-H., & Mota, C. M. M. (2012). A Multi-Attribute Decision Model for Portfolio Selection Aiming to Replace Technologies in Industrial Motor Systems. *Energy Conversion and Management*, *57*, 97–106. doi:10.1016/j.enconman.2011.12.013

Varun, B., & Prakashb, R. (2009). LCA of renewable energy for electricity generation systems—A review. *Renewable & Sustainable Energy Reviews*, *13*(5), 1067–1073. doi:10.1016/j.rser.2008.08.004

Weisser, D. (2007). A guide to life-cycle greenhouse gas (GHG) emissions from electric supply technologies. *Energy Volume*, *32*(9), 1543–1559. doi:10.1016/j.energy.2007.01.008

Zabalza Bribián, I., Aranda Usón, A., & Scarpellini, S. (2009). Life cycle assessment in buildings: State-of-the-art and simplified LCA methodology as a complement for building certification. *Building and Environment*, *44*(12), 2510–2520. doi:10.1016/j.buildenv.2009.05.001

ENDNOTE

[1]   Increase of employment

Chapter 3
An Intelligent Decision Support System for Sustainable Energy Local Planning

ABSTRACT

The main scope of this chapter is to present the "Action³" Decision Support System that integrates the MPC⁺ approach (Map - Plan - Choose - Check), supporting local and regional authorities to the development, implementation and monitoring of the Sustainable Energy and Climate Action Plan (especially within the framework of the Covenant of Mayors). The proposed intelligent system integrates three main modules, namely the "BEI-Action" for the development of the baseline emission inventory, the "MDS-Action" for the creation and evaluation of the alternative Scenarios of Actions aiming at the identification of the most promising Scenario, as well as the "SEC-Action" for the application of the "Methodological Approach for Monitoring SEC (Sustainable Energy Communities) Targets". The system was developed using the "Java" programming language and the "NetBeans IDE" software development platform. Particular emphasis was laid on the system's design, so as to be user-friendly, combining intuitive menus and navigation throughout the steps of the system.

DOI: 10.4018/978-1-5225-2286-7.ch003

INTRODUCTION

Sustainable energy policy has been a challenge for the local and regional authorities (EU, 2013). The disengagement from the unilateral economic development may be achieved through the progressive dissemination of renewable energy and rational use of energy actions. As a result, the decision making problem of the development and monitoring of the Sustainable Energy and Climate Action Plan (especially within the framework of Covenant of Mayors initiative) is an important component in local authorities' operation towards the creation of sustainable energy communities (Marinakis et al., 2017).

The "MPC$^+$ (Map - Plan - Choose - Check)" approach, presented in the previous Chapter, provides an integrated framework for the local energy planning, making available to the local authorities methods and tools for the development, implementation and monitoring of the Sustainable Energy and Climate Action Plan. In this context, the main scope of this Chapter is to present the "Action^3" information system that integrates the MPC$^+$ approach.

Step by step, the "Action^3" information system guide the local authorities in the required data entry in order to develop the municipality's Sustainable Energy Acton Plan. From filling in the community's general characteristics, up to the compilation of more complicated data, such as the Baselines Emission Inventory and the identification of Action Plan's activities, the system's stepwise approach is simple, concise and comprehensive. Its embedded modules can even support the decision maker during the procedure of monitoring the Action Plan's targets set.

More specifically, the structure of the proposed system is divided into three main modules, each divided into more steps:

- **"BEI-Action (Baseline Emission Inventory)" Module:** Identification of the current status of the municipality, integrating the individual algorithms for the alternative methods of energy balance' and of CO_2 emission factors' calculation, in order to develop the baseline emissions inventory.
- **"MDS-Action (Multicriteria Decision Support)" Module:** Design and creation of alternative Scenarios of Actions and assessment regarding the level of CO_2 emissions reduction. All the feasible Scenarios are evaluated using the multi-criteria analysis and robustness

analysis of the evaluation model, in order to identify the most promising Scenario for the examined municipality.

- **"SEC-Action (Sustainable Energy Communities)" Module:** Implementation of the Methodological Approach for Monitoring SEC Targets, aiming at the monitoring of the Sustainable Energy and Climate Action Plan implemented by the municipality and the relevant targets set.

Apart from the introduction, this Chapter is structured along five sections. Section 2 provides a description of the technologies used for the development of the "Action3" information system. Sections 3-5 are devoted to the presentation of the functionalities and front-end environments of the three modules "BEI-Action", "MDS-Action" and "SEC-Action". Finally, the last section just summarizes the key issues that have arisen in this paper.

TECHNOLOGIES

The information system was developed using the "Java" programming language and the "NetBeans IDE" software development platform. More specifically, the following technologies were required: technology for the development of graphical user interface, command and communication functions with ".xlsx" and ".xml" files, functions for ".pdf" files handling and generation, functions for graphs, functions for polynomial approximation and linear programming problem solving. In addition, the main "Java" libraries used, are the following:

- itextpdf-5.4.5 (creation and handling .pdf files).
- jdom-2.0.5 & dom4j-1.6.1 (creation and manipulation of files .xml).
- xmlbeans-2.3.0 (creation and manipulation of files .xml).
- jfreechart-1.0.17 & jcommon-1.0.21 (creation and operation diagrams).
- Commons-math3-3.2 (solving linear programming problems).
- poi-3.9 (handling files .xlsx).
- jasypt-1.9.2 (encryption and decryption).

First of all, the log in or sign in window is displayed to the end-user. With the entry of the end-users, an introductory window is displayed (Figure 1), which includes the following features:

Figure 1. User environment

- Selection of the available municipalities.
- Ability to add a new municipality.
- The "File" menu further enable the introduction of an ".xlsx" file with the data of a municipality, in order to add the municipality in the system.

Following the registration and selection of a record, the system makes available to the end-user the three main subsystems "BEI-Action", "MDS-Action" and "SEC-Action" (Figure 2).

"BEI-ACTION" MODULE

The main objective of the "BEI-Action" module is the development of the energy balance and baseline emission inventory. First of all, the end-user is asked to fill in the general characteristics of the municipality and select the baseline year and the target year.

Selecting the individual activity sectors of the municipality, the end-user is able to add the relevant data in the forms. In Figure 3, the end-user is inserting to the system the municipality's related energy consumptions in all activity sectors. It should be clarified that in order the Sustainable Energy and Climate Action Plan to be considered eligible, data should be submitted for three out of four of the following categories: "Municipal Buildings, Equipment

Figure 2. Main menu

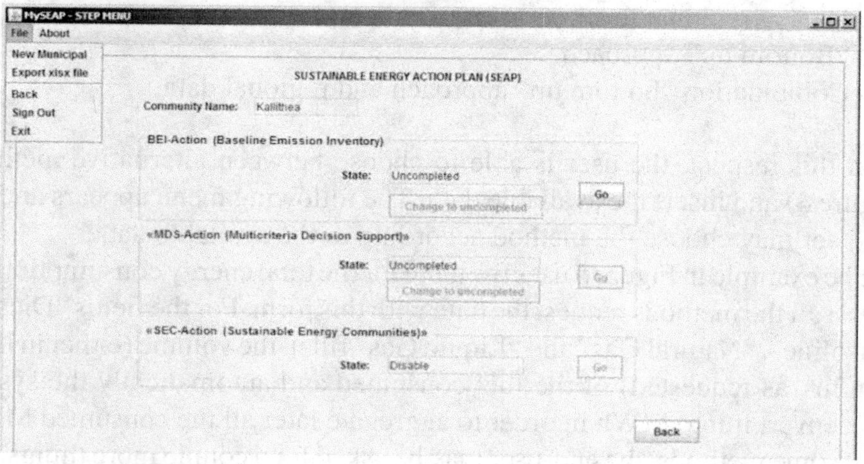

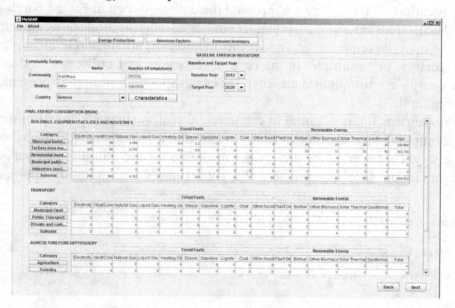

Figure 3. Final energy consumption

/ Facilities", "Residential Buildings", "Tertiary Buildings, Equipment/ Facilities" and "Transport".

The relevant algorithms of the following alternative methods for the final energy consumption calculation in each activity sector have been developed and integrated in the system.

- Total consumption.
- Data at regional level.
- "Bottom up" approach.
- Combination "bottom up" approach and regional data.

In this respect, the user is able to choose between alternative methods (Figure 4) and insert the available data. The following menu appears and the end-user may choose the method according to the available data.

The example in Figure 5 uses the table for the total energy consumption but almost all the methods request the data with this form. For the fields "Diesel", "Gasoline", "Natural Gas" and "Liquid Gas" fill in the volume (either in liters or in m^3, as requested) of the fuel consumed and automatically the system will convert it into MWh in order to aggregate later all the consumed MWh.

In some methods, the end-user may be asked for a couple more things. For example, if the "Bottom Up Approach" is chosen, where detailed registry of the consumptions is engaged, the end-user should define the category and the location of the facility and provide the data as shown in Figure 6 below.

The Bottom Up approach is mainly envisaged when accurate disaggregated data exist. The required data under this method slightly differentiate among the sectors. For example, in the case of the municipal buildings, it allows the energy consumption data entry for each separate building as presented in Figure 6.

As regards the residential or commercial sector, since separate building consumption data are not available, data entry is realized for the whole category. However, since data is not available for the building category at the municipal level (if available the Total Energy Consumption approach

Figure 4. Available data for the final energy consumption

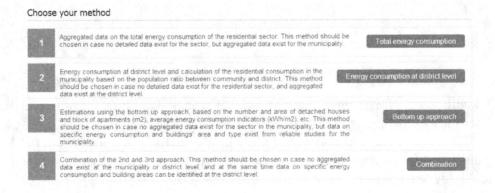

Figure 5. Total energy consumption separated per type of energy

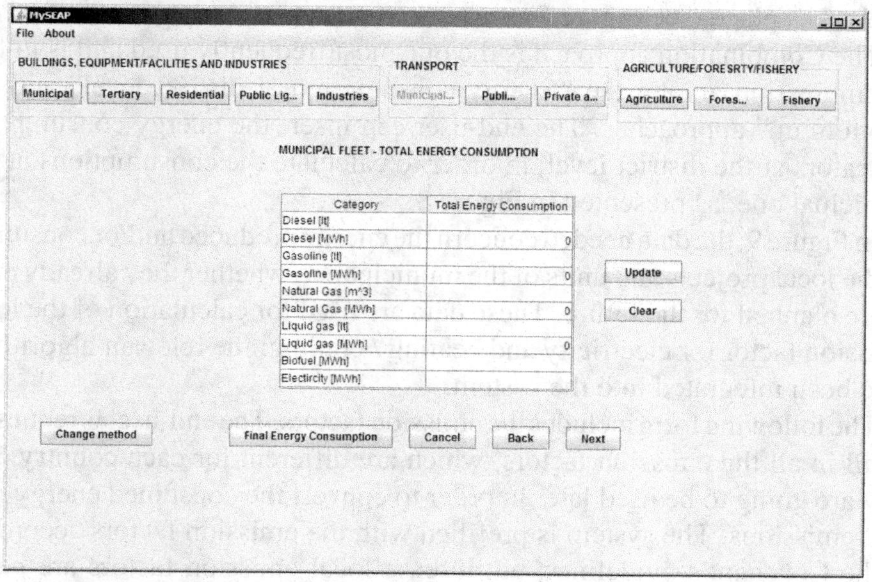

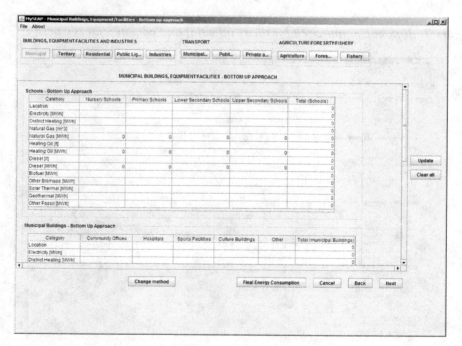

Figure 6. Bottom up approach for the municipal sector

should be selected), the use of specific energy indicators at the municipal level takes place (see Figure 7).

The Combination approach is the one most frequently used and is in fact a combination among the "Energy consumption at district level" and the "Bottom up" approaches. The end-user can insert the energy consumption indicators at the district level, in order to calculate the consumptions at the municipal one, as presented in Figure 8.

In Figure 9, the data needed concern the energy produced and/or consumed by the local projects and units of the municipality, whether they already exist or are planned for the future. These data are used for calculation of the local emission factor for electricity and heating / cooling; the relevant algorithms have been integrated into the system.

The following form includes the emission factors. The end-user is requested to fill in all the emission factors, which are different for each country, and they are going to be used later in order to convert the consumed energy into CO_2 emissions. The system is prefilled with the emission factors according to the Covenant's guidelines, but in case local emission factors are being used, or national electricity emission factors different from the guidelines, they should be entered at this stage (Figure 10).

Figure 7. Bottom Up approach for the residential and commercial sectors

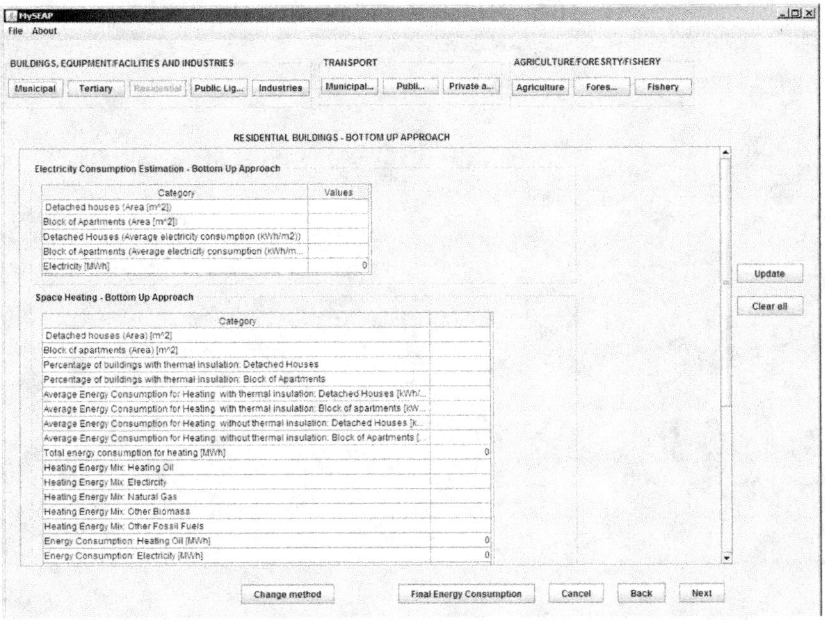

Figure 8. Combination approach

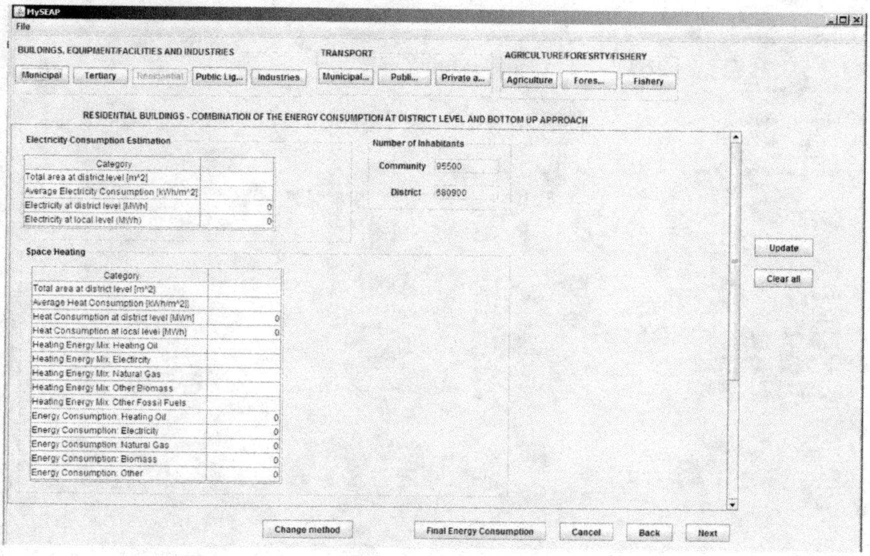

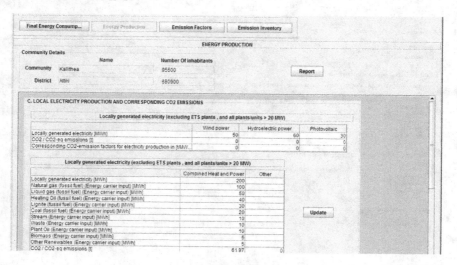

Figure 9. Local energy production

As depicted in Figure 11, the system has already converted all the consumed energy given in previous step, according to the emission factors, into tons of CO_2 emitted. Moreover, the sum of CO_2 emitted from each fuel/energy source but also the total CO_2 emissions from all the energy sources are displayed.

Figure 10. Emissions factors

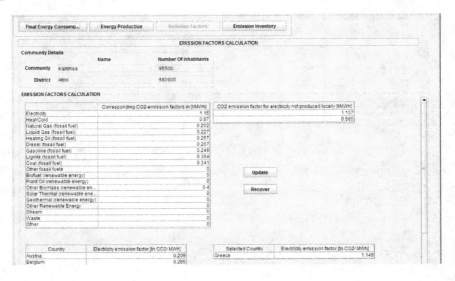

Figure 11. Baseline emission inventory

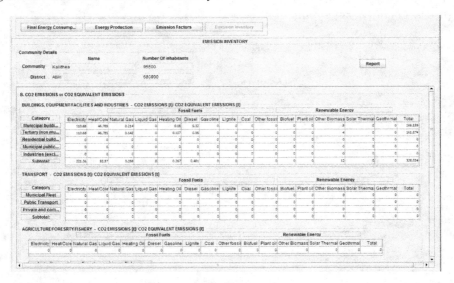

"MDS-ACTION" MODULE

The main objective of the subsystem "MDS-Action" is the design of alternative Scenarios of Actions, taking into consideration the modelling process, the participatory approach, the future estimated progress of the municipality consumptions and CO_2 reductions and the aspiration levels (CO_2 emissions reduction level achieved). Figure 12 shows the alternative Scenarios created by the system.

The criteria values are calculated for each Scenario of Actions. These values are based on the modelling process. However, the end-user is able to view and edit the available Scenarios, as well as to add new Scenarios of Actions. The end-user has the opportunity to take a look at the future estimated progress of the municipality consumptions and CO_2 reductions according to the data provided in all the previous steps. It is evaluated whether the selected combination of actions and their potential to cover the community's needs and aims in the medium and long term are enough or not. Whether the combination is successful depends on the possibility of achieving the target of at least 20% CO_2 reduction by 2020 or 40% CO_2 reduction by 2030.

Some external parameters are required for the future estimated progress, such as the population growth at national and municipal level and the annual heating and cooling degree days. In the figure 13 below, the end-user has a general view of how the tabs of this action look.

The end-user is provided with ideas and suggestions on how to engage the different kinds of stakeholders in the implementation of the Sustainable

Figure 12. Creation of alternative scenarios of actions

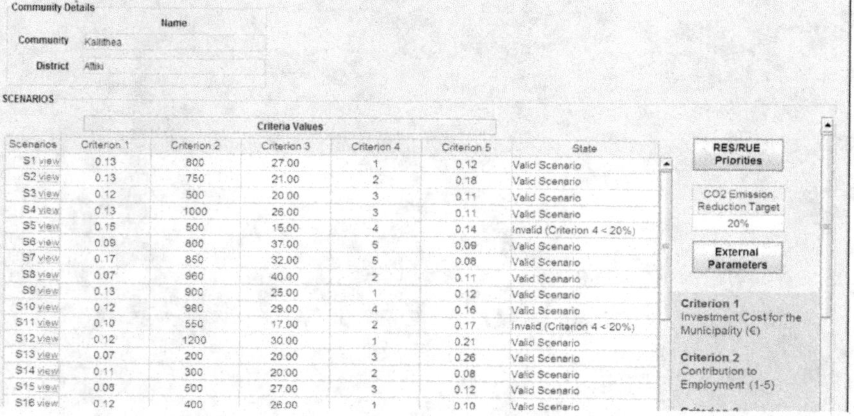

Figure 13. Data input

SELECTION OF SCENARIOS							

Community Details

Community	Kallithea	Name	
District	Attiki		

SCENARIOS

	Criteria Values						
Scenarios	Criterion 1	Criterion 2	Criterion 3	Criterion 4	Criterion 5	State	
S1 view	0.13	800	27.00	1	0.12	Valid Scenario	
S2 view	0.13	750	21.00	2	0.18	Valid Scenario	
S3 view	0.12	500	20.00	3	0.11	Valid Scenario	
S4 view	0.13	1000	26.00	3	0.11	Valid Scenario	
S5 view	0.15	500	15.00	4	0.14	Invalid (Criterion 4 < 20%)	
S6 view	0.09	800	37.00	5	0.09	Valid Scenario	
S7 view	0.17	850	32.00	5	0.08	Valid Scenario	
S8 view	0.07	960	40.00	2	0.11	Valid Scenario	
S9 view	0.13	900	26.00	1	0.12	Valid Scenario	
S10 view	0.12	980	29.00	4	0.16	Valid Scenario	
S11 view	0.10	550	17.00	2	0.17	Invalid (Criterion 4 < 20%)	
S12 view	0.12	1200	30.00	1	0.21	Valid Scenario	
S13 view	0.07	200	20.00	3	0.26	Valid Scenario	
S14 view	0.11	300	20.00	2	0.08	Valid Scenario	
S15 view	0.08	500	27.00	3	0.12	Valid Scenario	
S16 view	0.12	400	26.00	1	0.10	Valid Scenario	

RES/RUE Priorities

CO2 Emission Reduction Target
20%

External Parameters

Criterion 1
Investment Cost for the Municipality (€)

Criterion 2
Contribution to Employment (1-5)

Energy and Climate Action Plan ("RES/RUE Priorities"). All the presented ideas have already been implemented in several municipalities all over Europe, and therefore constitute best practices. It contains info on who exactly are the stakeholders and displays also some related material (Pepesec Stakeholder Engagement Methodology and Application of Stakeholders Engagement Methodology) with further information on their engagement in projects concerning the energy planning of a municipality, as shown in Figure 14.

Moreover, the end-user can take some ideas from other municipalities that have tried successfully to teach the stakeholders about their Action Plan's implementation and renewable energy and rational use of energy projects. The

Figure 14. Methods for the stakeholders' engagement

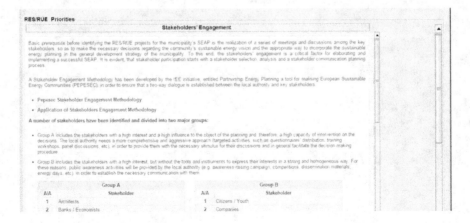

user can read solid examples on how other municipalities achieved to raise the public awareness and make their citizens more self-conscious about the energy they consume and the new projects in the area. It is like a short library of ideas for the new communities that are aiming to become sustainable, as well as communities already on the way.

Initially, the user is given access to a huge library of renewable energy and rational use of energy projects that are already implemented in different areas in Europe. Over 100 projects described in detail exist in this library. The end-user can click on the option "View Details" on some project in order to access a specific page with detailed data about it (e.g. location, time of construction, cost etc.) including a brief introductory text (Figure 15). There are several filters to make the search easier to find a specific project ("Cate gory"/"Type"/"Country"/"Scale"/"Community").

In the first stage, all Scenarios are evaluated based on the level of CO_2 emissions reduction. The long-term target is entered by the end-user ("CO_2 Emission Reduction Target" field). Therefore, according to the deviation of the estimated emissions reduction compared with the long-term target, the status of each Scenario is presented in the column "State" (Figure 12). In this respect, the feasible Scenarios of Actions can be also displayed in a chart (Figure 16).

The end-user provides the criteria values for the creation of the marginal value factions (Figure 17).

The regression line that best fits the points set by the end-user is created, based on a polynomial approach. The required polynomial approach was implemented by the following findPolynomial () method of the Calculations class.

Figure 15. Database of renewable energy and rational use of energy projects

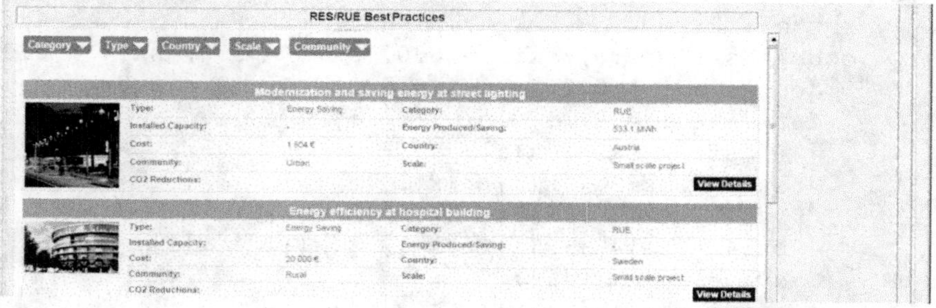

Figure 16. Feasible scenarios of actions

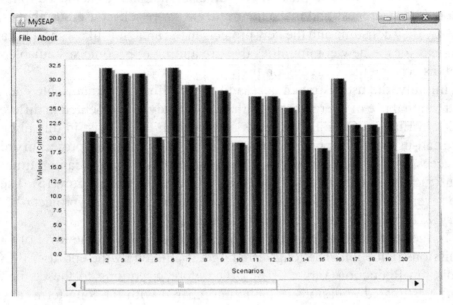

Figure 17. Criteria values in order to generate marginal value factions

Criteria Values (Qualitative X% / Quantitative)	Criterion 1	Criterion 3	Criterion 4	Criterion 5	Criterion 6
0% / 1	0	0	0	0	0
20% / 2	0.40	0.20	0.20	0.35	0.50
40% / 3	0.50	0.40	0.25	0.70	0.60
60% / 4	0.70	0.80	0.70	0.80	0.80
80% / -	0.90		0.80	0.90	
100% / 5	1	1	1	1	1

Clear

```
1. public double[] findPolynomial(double[] x, double[] y) {
2.     double[] sol = new double[3];
3.     try {
4.       int n = 6;
5.       double sxi = 0.0, sxi2 = 0.0, sxi3 = 0.0, sxi4 = 0.0;
6.       double syi = 0.0, syixi = 0.0, syixi2 = 0.0;
7.       for (int i = 0; i < n; i++) {
8.           sxi = sxi + x[i];
9.         sxi2 = sxi2 + x[i] * x[i];
10.        sxi3 = sxi3 + x[i] * x[i] * x[i];
11.        sxi4 = sxi4 + x[i] * x[i] * x[i] * x[i];
12.        syi = syi + y[i];
13.        syixi = syixi + y[i] * x[i];
14.        syixi2 = syixi2 + y[i] * x[i] * x[i];
15.      }
```

```
16.          LinearObjectiveFunction f = new
             LinearObjectiveFunction(
17.            new double[]{0.0, 0.0, 0.0}, 0.0);
18.          Collection<LinearConstraint> constraints =
19.               new ArrayList<>();
20.          constraints.add(new LinearConstraint(
21.            new double[]{n, sxi, sxi2}, Relationship.EQ, syi));
22.          constraints.add(new LinearConstraint(
23.            new double[]{sxi, sxi2, sxi3},
24.              Relationship.EQ, syixi));
25.          constraints.add(new LinearConstraint(
26.            new double[]{sxi2, sxi3, sxi4},
27.              Relationship.EQ, syixi2));
28.          SimplexSolver solver = new SimplexSolver();
29.          PointValuePair optSolution = solver.optimize(
30.            new MaxIter(100), f,
31.            new LinearConstraintSet(constraints),
32.          · GoalType.MINIMIZE,
33.            new NonNegativeConstraint(false));
34.          sol = optSolution.getPoint();
35.          return sol;
36.            } catch (TooManyIterationsException e) {
37.            System.out.println(
38.              "Calculations.findPolynomial: returned null");
39.            return null;
40.          }
41.     }
42.}
```

For the construction of the reference set $A_R = \{a_1, a_2, ..., a_m\}$, by the analyst, virtual Scenarios are selected. The relevant form of the system is displayed in Figure 18.

Finally, the linear program is solved for the calculation of the criteria weights. The linearProgrammingCalculator10 () method of the Calculations class is used to solve the linear program.

```
1. public double[] linearProgrammingCalculator10(
2.         int count, double[][] gs, double d) {
3.       try {
4.     double[][] a = new double[count][10];
5.     for (int i = 0; i < count; i++) {
6.       for (int j = 0; j < 10; j++) {
7.         if (j < 6) {
8.           a[i][j] = gs[i][j];
9.         } else if (j == 6 || j == 8) {
10.            a[i][j] = -1.0;
```

Figure 18. Reference scenarios

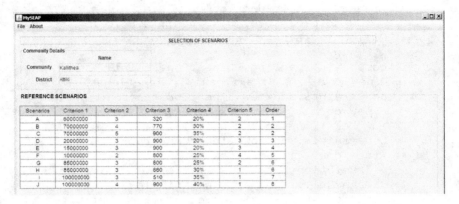

Scenarios	Criterion 1	Criterion 2	Criterion 3	Criterion 4	Criterion 5	Order
A	80000000	3	320	20%	2	1
B	70000000	4	770	30%	2	2
C	70000000	5	900	35%	2	2
D	20000000	3	900	20%	3	3
E	15000000	3	900	20%	3	4
F	10000000	2	800	25%	4	5
G	85000000	3	800	25%	2	6
H	85000000	3	660	30%	1	6
I	100000000	3	510	35%	1	7
J	100000000	4	900	40%	1	8

```
11.             } else {
12.                a[i][j] = 1.0;
13.             }
14.          }
15.       }
16.       LinearObjectiveFunction f = new LinearObjectiveFunction(
17.          new double[]{0.0, 0.0, 0.0, 0.0, 0.0,
18.             0.0, 1.0, 1.0, 1.0, 1.0}, 0.0);
19.       Collection<LinearConstraint> constraints = new ArrayList<>();
20.       for (int i = 0; i < count; i++) {
21.          if (gs[i][6] > 0) {
22.             constraints.add(
23.               new LinearConstraint(
24.               new double[]{gs[i][0], gs[i][1], gs[i][2],
25.                  gs[i][3], gs[i][4], gs[i][5], -1.0,
26.                  1.0, -1.0, 1.0}, Relationship.GEQ, d));
27.          } else {
28.             constraints.add(
29.               new LinearConstraint(
30.               new double[]{gs[i][0], gs[i][1], gs[i][2],
31.                  gs[i][3], gs[i][4], gs[i][5],
32.                  -1.0, 1.0, -1.0, 1.0},
33.                  Relationship.EQ, 0.0));
34.          }
35.       }
36.       ///pi >= 0
37.       constraints.add(
38.          new LinearConstraint(
39.          new double[]{1.0, 0.0, 0.0, 0.0, 0.0, 0.0,
40.             0.0, 0.0, 0.0, 0.0}, Relationship.GEQ, 0.0));
41.       constraints.add(
42.          new LinearConstraint(
```

```
43.              new double[]{0.0, 1.0, 0.0, 0.0, 0.0, 0.0, 0.0,
44.                 0.0, 0.0, 0.0}, Relationship.GEQ, 0.0));
45.          constraints.add(
46.              new LinearConstraint(
47.              new double[]{0.0, 0.0, 1.0, 0.0, 0.0, 0.0, 0.0,
48.                 0.0, 0.0, 0.0}, Relationship.GEQ, 0.0));
49.          constraints.add(
50.              new LinearConstraint(
51.              new double[]{0.0, 0.0, 0.0, 1.0, 0.0, 0.0, 0.0,
52.                 0.0, 0.0, 0.0}, Relationship.GEQ, 0.0));
53.          constraints.add(
54.              new LinearConstraint(
55.              new double[]{0.0, 0.0, 0.0, 0.0, 1.0, 0.0, 0.0, 0.0,
56.                 0.0, 0.0}, Relationship.GEQ, 0.0));
57.          constraints.add(
58.              new LinearConstraint(
59.              new double[]{0.0, 0.0, 0.0, 0.0, 0.0, 1.0, 0.0, 0.0,
60.                 0.0, 0.0}, Relationship.GEQ, 0.0));
61.          ///sa+ >= 0, sa- >= 0, sb+ >= 0, sb- >= 0
62.          constraints.add(
63.              new LinearConstraint(
64.              new double[]{0.0, 0.0, 0.0, 0.0, 0.0, 0.0, 1.0, 0.0,
65.                 0.0, 0.0}, Relationship.GEQ, 0.0));
66.          constraints.add(
67.              new LinearConstraint(
68.              new double[]{0.0, 0.0, 0.0, 0.0, 0.0, 0.0, 0.0, 1.0,
69.                 0.0, 0.0}, Relationship.GEQ, 0.0));
70.          constraints.add(
71.              new LinearConstraint(
71.              new double[]{0.0, 0.0, 0.0, 0.0, 0.0, 0.0, 0.0, 0.0,
72.                 1.0, 0.0}, Relationship.GEQ, 0.0));
73.          constraints.add(
74.              new LinearConstraint(
75.              new double[]{0.0, 0.0, 0.0, 0.0, 0.0, 0.0, 0.0, 0.0,
76.                 0.0, 1.0}, Relationship.GEQ, 0.0));
77.          //Sum(pi)=1
78.          constraints.add(
79.              new LinearConstraint(
80.              new double[]{1.0, 1.0, 1.0, 1.0, 1.0, 1.0, 0.0, 0.0,
81.                 0.0, 0.0}, Relationship.EQ, 1.0));
82.          SimplexSolver solver = new SimplexSolver();
83.          PointValuePair optSolution = solver.optimize(
84.              new MaxIter(100), f,
85.              new LinearConstraintSet(constraints),
86.              GoalType.MINIMIZE,
87.              new NonNegativeConstraint(true));
88.          double[] sol=new double[10];
89.          sol = optSolution.getPoint();
90.          return sol;
```

```
91.        } catch (Exception e) {
92.          System.out.println(
93.            "Calculations.linearProgrammingCalculator10: "
94.            + "returned null");
95.          return null;
96.        }
97.      }
```

Following the calculation of the weights, the ranking table of the alternative Scenarios of Actions is presented. The scenarios are arranged in descending order according to their final value (Figure 19). Moreover, the results from the robustness analysis can be displayed, namely the maximum and minimum position that each alternative Scenario can get in the ranking.

"SEC-ACTION" MODULE

On the "SEC-Action" module, the end-user is given the opportunity to monitor the results of the Action Plan by constructing a new emission inventory for the monitoring year and by monitoring the actions' progress. The front-end environment of the monitoring of the progress Action Plan's implementation include the following (Figure 20):

- Main window, for the selection of the evaluation year ("Monitoring Records").
- The user is led to previous forms of the system ("Monitoring Data"), in order to provide data on the energy balance and baseline emissions inventory, as well as on the progress of the actions' and measures' implementation.

Figure 19. Problem solve

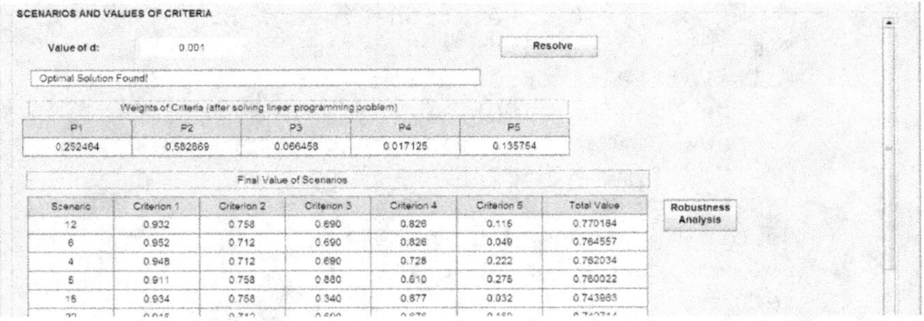

Figure 20. Monitoring of the action plan

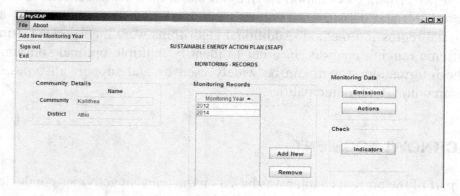

- Based on the provided data, the calculation of the monitoring indicators and the "SEC_{Index}" take place, both for each activity sector and the whole municipality.

CONCLUSION

The proposed information system "Action³", integrating the MPC⁺ approach (Map - Plan - Choose - Check)», can support local authorities to the selection of the most appropriate combination of renewable energy and rational use of energy actions at local - regional level. This Chapter provided a detailed description of the "BEI-Action", "MDS-Action" and "SEC-Action" modules for the implementation of the local energy planning.

More specifically, a number of renewable energy and rational use of energy actions can be identified for the agricultural, public, tertiary and residential sector, as well as transport and local energy production. Efforts were also focused on the adoption of cities' and local/regional communities' specific characteristics. Using data from the end-users and indicators from the international literature and reports, these actions take an "editable" form.

An initial design of alternative Scenarios take place according to the range of the actions' application in each sector, as well as techniques of participatory planning and aspiration levels. Following the alternative scenarios' creation, their performance evaluation carried out based on a set of criteria, as well as a direct and transparent additive value model which is assessed by an ordinal regression method. Additional algorithms were incorporated using extreme ranking analysis, in order to identify multiple optimal solutions. The information system can be widely used by and support all types of communities and municipalities.

ACKNOWLEDGMENT

A part of the current chapter was based on the relevant activities conducted within the framework of the project "Rural Web Energy Learning Network for Action – eReNet (Project no: IEE/10/224/SI2.593412), supported by the Intelligent Energy – Europe (IEE) Programme. The content of the chapter is the sole responsibility of its author and does not necessary reflect the views of the EC.

REFERENCES

EU - European Union. (2013). *Delivering on the Europe 2020 Strategy: Handbook for Local and Regional Authorities*. Brussels, Belgium: Committee of the Regions.

Marinakis, V., Papadopoulou, A., & Psarras, J. (2017). Local Communities towards a Sustainable Energy Future: Needs and Priorities. *International Journal of Sustainable Energy*, *36*(3), 296–312. doi:10.1080/14786451.2015.1018264

Chapter 4
Developing and Monitoring a Sustainable Energy and Climate Action Plan for an Energy–Producing Community

ABSTRACT

The development, implementation and monitoring of the Sustainable Energy and Climate Action Plan require a significant amount of data and analysis, as well as an effective and comprehensive decision making process. This chapter presents the pilot application of the proposed "MPC+ (Map - Plan - Choose - Check)" framework, through the "Action³" Decision Support System, in a Greek energy-producing community. The pilot application is conducted in three phases, namely the development of the baseline emission inventory (Phase I), the creation and evaluation of alternative Scenarios of Actions (Phase II) and the monitoring of the actions and measures implemented (Phase III). The city's univocal economy orientation of energy production through lignite is considered as a basic, inhibitory factor towards sustainability. In this respect, the city has committed to implement a series of appropriate renewable energy and rational use of energy activities in its territory, laying balanced emphasis on the local energy and heat production, and the promotion and implementation of measures on energy savings. A significant part of the CO_2 emissions' reduction will come from the installation of biomass district heating systems in local communities.

DOI: 10.4018/978-1-5225-2286-7.ch004

INTRODUCTION

The aim of this Chapter is to present the pilot application of the proposed approach "MPC+ (Map - Plan - Choose - Check)", through the information system "Action³", in a Greek municipality. More specifically, the MPC+ approach has been applied to the Municipality of Amyntaio, Greece, during the development of its Sustainable Energy Action Plan within the framework of the Covenant of Mayors.

The Municipality of Amyntaio has proceeded to the adoption of a series of initiatives and actions by 2020, taking into consideration that the local authorities' role is not limited to the provision of public services to citizens, but they ought to operate as a political, social and development body. The first step towards this direction was implemented through the Municipality's participation in the Network of Energy Producing Municipalities (NEProM). NEProM includes the five Greek Municipalities, where PPC has established and operates thermal power stations for electricity production through lignite. The Network's strategic objectives include the environmental protection of the particular areas, as well as the local economies' and societies' smooth transition to the post-lignite period, through the promotion of alternative technologies. The Mayor and municipal council of Amyntaio, exhibiting their strong political will and commitment towards sustainable energy planning, adhered to the Covenant of Mayors (CoM) on the 18th April of 2011.

The pilot application of the proposed approach "MPC+ (Map - Plan - Choose - Check)", through the information system "Action³", is conducted in three phases, as shown in Figure 1.

Phase I: Baseline emission inventory.
Phase II: Creation and evaluation of alternative scenarios.
Phase III: Monitoring.

Apart from the introduction, this Chapter is structured along four sections. Sections 2-4 provide the results from the application of the MPC+ approach to the Greek municipality, namely the development of the baseline emission inventory (Phase 1), the creation and evaluation of alternative Scenarios of Actions (Phase 2) and the monitoring of Action Plan implemented (Phase 3). Finally, the last section just summarizes the key issues that have arisen in this paper.

Figure 1. Pilot application phases

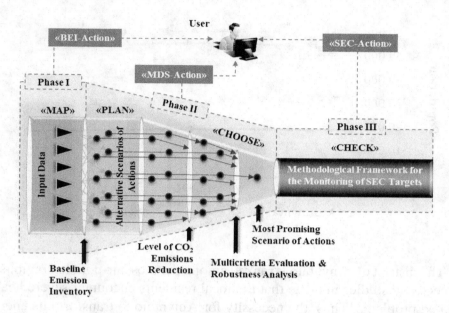

PHASE I: BASELINE EMISION INVENTORY

Characteristics

The Municipality of Amyntaio is located in the southern part of the district of Florina and has an area of 58.932,3 ha. Ayntaio is a municipality in the prefecture of Florina in Macedonia, Greece and consists of six municipal units, namely Aetos, Amyntaio, Variko, Lechovo, Nymfaio and Filotas. The total population was 16.890 inhabitants in 2011. The population of the municipality remained at the same level for the period 1991 – 2001, as shown in Figure 2, increased compared to 2011 (Figure 2).

The agricultural sector is characterized by a strong orientation to arable crops. The vineyard plays also an important role in the Municipality of Amyntaio.

Due to its richness in lignite, a Lignite-Fired Power Plant is operating in Amyntaio which consists of two units of 300 MW each. These units are part of the largest Greek Lignite Production Center established in the Ptolemais-Amyntaio district, where there are 16 generating units in function with a total capacity of 4,050 MW. Furthermore, in the surrounding area four mines are currently operating, and supply the nearest plants with lignite.

Figure 2. Population

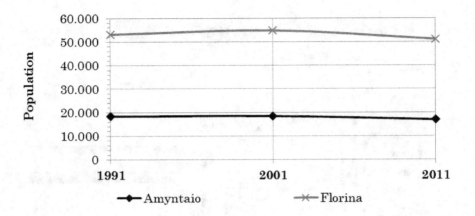

The district of Amyntaio is ranked among the most air-polluted regions in Greece and studies indicate that the local residents encounter severe health related problems. Thus, the necessity for Amyntaio to transform its energy profile in a more sustainable one is more than evident. These necessities have to be directly linked with the constant and stable employment of local citizens. Moreover, the severely suffering from financial and economic crisis Greek municipality is in need for development opportunities, such as those arising from sustainable energy prospects.

Baseline Emission Inventory

The selected inventory year for the Municipality of Amyntaio is 2009. The Baseline Emission Inventory is based on "standard" emissions factors in line with the Intergovernmental Panel on Climate Change (IPCC) principles. This approach is based on the carbon content of each fuel, like in national greenhouse gas inventories in the context of the United Nations Framework Convention on Climate Change (UNFCCC) and the Kyoto protocol.

- **Agricultural Sector:** The primary sector's activities lead to high energy consumption and include the operation of pumps for irrigation; use of tractors; operation of livestock. The total diesel consumption of the agricultural sector is estimated at 35.662 MWh and the electricity consumption at 21.628 MWh;

- **Municipal Buildings and Equipment/Facilities:** This category includes all buildings operated by the municipality, such as nurseries, schools, offices, old people's homes, sport facilities, etc. Moreover, it includes municipal facilities related to water supply, irrigation and sewage treatment. Electricity, heating oil (4.650 MWh) and district heating (1.523 MWh) are used for heating. Electricity (4.498 MWh) is used also for lighting, cooling, as well as electrical and mechanical equipment.
- **Residential Buildings:** See below:
  - **Electricity:** The electricity consumption of the residential sector is 19.538.420 kWh, based on the available data from the Public Power Corporation (PPC);
  - **Heat:** The heating oil, wood, district heating and electricity are used for heating in the residential buildings of Amyntaio. The energy consumption was calculated using a "bottom-up" approach, namely existing statistical data, specific energy consumption indicators and relevant studies:
    - **District Heating:** Based on the available data from DETEPA, the energy consumption was 18.461.569 kWh in 2009;
    - **Heating Oil:** The calculation of heating oil consumption is based on the available data from the Hellenic Statistical Authority (EL.STAT.) and the Municipality of Amyntaio regarding the area of residential buildings. The needs for thermal comfort of residential buildings with central heating using heating oil and district heating is estimated at 101.689.385 kWh. Taking into consideration the fuel poverty, especially in rural areas with high thermal comfort needs, the actual energy consumption is estimated at 75% of the calculated thermal needs, as the population does not fully satisfy the conditions of thermal comfort. This result is based on the relevant study of EL.STAT. regarding living conditions in Greece and poverty level in 2009, which affects 27,6% of the population. Therefore, the total actual energy demand in the residential buildings with central heating is estimated at 76.267.038 kWh. Deducting district heating energy consumption and using an average efficiency of 85% for central heating systems, the estimated consumption of heating oil is 68.006.434 kWh. According to a relevant study of the National Observatory of Athens and the available data

of EL.STAT., the residential buildings with other form of heating use 37,5% oil stoves, 50% electricity and 12,5% open hearth fireplaces. In this context, the heating oil consumption is estimated at 15.698.413 kWh;

- **Other Energy Sources:** Taking into consideration the above analysis, the energy consumption for the operation of open hearth fireplaces and air conditioners is estimated at 10.465.609 kWh of biomass and 11.016.430 kWh of electricity, respectively. The calculation of solar energy is based on a relevant study regarding the energy saving from solar panels' installation (6,6 KWh/m2) and the rate of installed solar panels on buildings (30%);

- **Tertiary (Non-Municipal) Buildings, Equipment/Facilities:** The electricity consumption of the tertiary sector is estimated at 15.181.493 kWh, based on the available data from PPC. The heating oil and district heating are used for the thermal needs of the tertiary sector. The heating oil consumption was calculated using the total heating oil consumption at the municipal level minus the relevant consumptions of the municipal and residential buildings. The total heating oil consumption data for Florina district was provided by the Directorate of Petroleum Policy, Ministry of Environment, Energy & Climate Change, while population ratios were used for the identification of heating oil consumption at the municipality level;

- **Municipal Public Lighting:** Concerning municipal public lighting, the data collection was based on the relevant PPC invoices for the Municipality. The electricity consumption is 2.073 MWh;

- **Municipal Fleet:** The Municipality of Amyntaio has a number of vehicles, used to meet the needs of transport, collection and disposal of waste, emergency medical needs and technical support. The consumption of diesel is 866.530 and gasoline 227.079 MWh;

- **Public Transport:** The energy consumption of the public transport was estimated using the available data from the operator of Florina bus station. In addition, the energy consumption of the school transport services (by buses) was taken also into consideration. The energy consumption (diesel) of the public transport is 1.266 MWh;

- **Private and Commercial Transport:** The energy consumption of the private and commercial transport is calculated using data from the Department of Petroleum Policy of the Ministry of Environment, Energy and Climate Change, as well as the number of vehicles per fuel type at district and municipal level from the Department of Organization and Informatics, Ministry of Development, Competitiveness, Infrastructure, Transport and Networks. The consumption of gasoline is 31.034 MWh and diesel 41.585 MWh.

According to the energy and baseline emission inventory, the municipality consumed 308,6 GWh ((18,3 MWh/capita) in 2009 (Figure 3).

The agricultural sector was responsible for 18.6%, the building sector and facilities for 57.1% and the transport sector for 24.3% of the total final energy consumption. The electricity consumption is estimated at 20.4%, district heating 8.9%, heating oil at 31.0%, diesel 25.7%, gasoline 10.1%, biomass 3.4% and solar thermal 0.5% of the total final energy consumption. This energy consumption led to 138.064,7 $tnCO_2$ (8,2 $tnCO_2$/resident).

The breakdown of final energy consumption and CO_2 emissions per type of consumption and energy is illustrated in Figures 4 and 5.

Local Electricity Production

The Municipality of Amyntaio is an "energy producing" municipality. However, the municipality includes in its SEAP the "small" local plants/units for power generation. More specifically, the following criteria were taken into consideration:

Figure 3. Baseline emission inventory

FINAL ENERGY CONSUMPTION [MWh]

BUILDINGS, EQUIPMENT/FACILITIES AND INDUSTRIES

			Fossil Fuels								Renewable Energy					
Category	Electricity	Heat/Cold	Natural Gas	Liquid Gas	Heating Oil	Diesel	Gasoline	Lignite	Coal	Other fossil	Plant Oil	Biofuel	Other Biomass	Solar Thermal	Geother	Total
Municipal buildi...	4 498,4	1 523,4	0,0	0,0	4 649,8	0,0	0,0	0,0	0,0	0,0	0,0	0,0	0,0	0,0	0,0	10 671,6
Tertiary (non mu...	15 181,5	7 367,4	0,0	0,0	7 323,4	0,0	0,0	0,0	0,0	0,0	0,0	0,0	0,0	0,0	0,0	29 872,3
Residential build...	19 538,4	18 461,6	0,0	0,0	83 704,8	0,0	0,0	0,0	0,0	0,0	0,0	0,0	10 465,6	1 429,8	0,0	133 600,2
Municipal public...	2 073,3	0,0	0,0	0,0	0,0	0,0	0,0	0,0	0,0	0,0	0,0	0,0	0,0	0,0	0,0	2 073,3
Industries (excl...	0,0	0,0	0,0	0,0	0,0	0,0	0,0	0,0	0,0	0,0	0,0	0,0	0,0	0,0	0,0	0,0
Subtotal:	41 291,6	27 352,4	0,0	0,0	95 678,0	0,0	0,0	0,0	0,0	0,0	0,0	0,0	10 465,6	1 429,8	0,0	176 217,4

FINAL ENERGY CONSUMPTION [MWh]

TRANSPORT

			Fossil Fuels								Renewable Energy					
Category	Electricity	Heat/Cold	Natural Gas	Liquid Gas	Heating Oil	Diesel	Gasoline	Lignite	Coal	Other fossil	Plant Oil	Biofuel	Other Biomass	Solar Thermal	Geother	Total
Municipal Fleet	0,0	0,0	0,0	0,0	0,0	866,5	246,3	0,0	0,0	0,0	0,0	0,0	0,0	0,0	0,0	1 112,9
Public Transport	0,0	0,0	0,0	0,0	0,0	1 265,9	0,0	0,0	0,0	0,0	0,0	0,0	0,0	0,0	0,0	1 265,9
Private and com...	0,0	0,0	0,0	0,0	0,0	41 584,8	31 033,5	0,0	0,0	0,0	0,0	0,0	0,0	0,0	0,0	72 618,3
Subtotal:	0,0	0,0	0,0	0,0	0,0	43 717,3	31 279,8	0,0	0,0	0,0	0,0	0,0	0,0	0,0	0,0	74 997,1

AGRICULTURE/FORESRTY/FISHERY

			Fossil Fuels								Renewable Energy					
Category	Electricity	Heat/Cold	Natural Gas	Liquid Gas	Heating Oil	Diesel	Gasoline	Lignite	Coal	Other fossil	Plant Oil	Biofuel	Other Biomass	Solar Thermal	Geother	Total
Agriculture	21 628,2	0,0	0,0	0,0	0,0	35 662,4	0,0	0,0	0,0	0,0	0,0	0,0	0,0	0,0	0,0	57 290,6
Forestry	0,0	0,0	0,0	0,0	0,0	0,0	0,0	0,0	0,0	0,0	0,0	0,0	0,0	0,0	0,0	0,0
Fishery	0,0	0,0	0,0	0,0	0,0	0,0	0,0	0,0	0,0	0,0	0,0	0,0	0,0	0,0	0,0	0,0
Subtotal:	21 628,2	0,0	0,0	0,0	0,0	35 662,4	0,0	0,0	0,0	0,0	0,0	0,0	0,0	0,0	0,0	57 290,6

Figure 4. Final energy consumption (left) and CO$_2$ emissions (right) per type of consumption

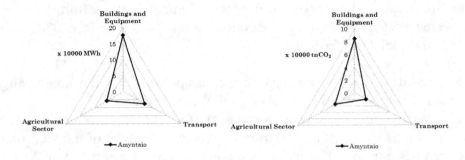

Figure 5. Final energy consumption (left) and CO$_2$ emissions (right) per type of energy

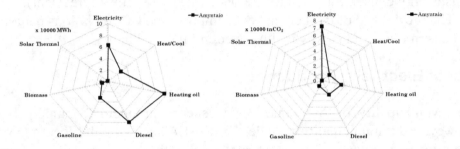

- Plants/units are not included in the European Emissions Trading Scheme (ETS);
- Plants/units are below or equal to 20 MW as thermal energy input in the case of fuel combustion plants, or output for renewable (20 MW corresponds to the EU ETS threshold for combustion installations).

A large amount of electricity is produced within the territory from the power station Amyntaio – Filotas, based on Combined Heat and Power (CHP). However, this plant is of high installed capacity (2x300 MW) and it is included in the ETS. For these reasons, its electricity production is not included in the SEAP.

The local electricity production from photovoltaic installations included in the SEAP is estimated at 352,8 MWh.

Local Heat/Cold Production

District heating is provided by DETEPA to the local communities of Amyntaio, Philota and Levaia, including a CHP unit Amyntaio-Philota. Even though the Steam Power Plant's (SPP) thermal capacity is higher than 20MW (24MWth), and the station is participating in the Greenhouse Gas Emissions Trading Scheme, thermal production was included in the municipality's SEAP, as the domectic, tertiaty and municipal sector's thermal needs are satisfied through district heating, provided by the particular power plant.

According to DETEPA's data, within 2009, 31.511 MWh were purchased by PPC, amount identical to the thermal power produced by the SPP, while the total consumption of the previously mentioned sectors was 27.352,4 MWh. Therefore, the district heating network's losses amount to 13,2% of the thermal energy produced, as no own consumption exists.

PHASE II: CREATION AND EVALUATION OF ALTERNATIVE SCENARIOS

Creation of Alternative Scenarios

For Amyntaio municipality, the decisive factor for the Action Plan's successful implementation is the active contribution of all local stakeholders (regional energy agencies, local chambers, producers of electricity and heat, citizens, members of the municipal council etc) for the configuration of local energy and environmental policies. Together, the local authorities and stakeholders can co-create the energy vision for the territory and the ways for its implementation, and invest financial and human resources towards this direction.

In this respect, two public consultation meetings on the Sustainable Energy and Climate Action Plan were realized, on June and October 2012. The first consultation was also realized within the framework of EUSEW2012, and in this respect had a number of informative discussions in its agenda on the Covenant and EU best practices. In the first consultation meeting the baseline emission inventory was presented, as well as some initial suggestions for renewable energy and rational use of energy actions and feedback from the stakeholders was received. Based on this, the Sustainable Energy and Climate Action Plan team updated the actions, which were presented in their final form in the 2nd consultation meeting. During this 2nd meeting, discussions were realized with all stakeholders. It should be noted that the Sustainable Energy and Climate Action Plan was approved on 17th of October 2012, unanimously.

The input data provided for the municipality (Figures 6) were used for the estimation of the future evolution of CO_2 emissions. The relevant forms include data such as the evolution of the municipal population, the heating and cooling degree days for the region and estimated the road network.

Furthermore, the data used for the evolution of the population at national level, changes in electricity prices and fuel, as well as change in energy consumption in individual sectors (primary, tertiary, home, industry, transport and agriculture) at national level are depicted in Figure 7.

Figure 6. Values of external parameters

INPUT

Inventory Year:	2010				
	Inventory Year	2015	2020	2025	2030
Population Growth (Municipal)	16.890	16.850	16.800	16.800	16.850
Population Growth (Municipal) (age 0-19)	1.050	1.000	950	950	950

Annual Heating Degree Days (Municipal)	2.584
Annual Cooling Degree Days (Municipal)	40

	2009 - 15	2015 - 20	2020 - 25	2025 - 30
Development of the road network (0-5)	1	1	1	1

Figure 7. Values of key parameters at national level

	Inventory Year	2015	2020	2025	2030
Population Growth (National) (x1.000)	11.316	11.505	11.618	11.674	11.699

Projection of Energy Consumption (ktoe)	Inventory Year	2015	2020	2025	2030
Agriculture	1.065	1.045	1.033	1.044	1.051
Indusrty	4.300	4.192	4.486	4.936	4.729
Transport	8.355	8.757	9.368	10.018	10.521
Residential	5.752	6.009	6.865	7.544	8.089
Tertiary	2.059	2.193	2.436	2.680	2.884

	Inventory Year	2015	2020	2025	2030
Per capita gross domestic product (€ per c...	18.101	18.769	21.151	23.400	26.135

Price rates	2015	2020	2025	2030
Electricity	0,1	0,1	0,1	0,1

	Inventory Year	2015	2020	2025	2030
Natural Gas	9,84	9,91	11,47	12,41	13,29
Crude Oil	91,94	86,68	100	107,5	115

It is noted that the change in energy consumption at national level resulting from the relevant study in Greece (ΥΠΕΚΑ, 2010b). Fuel prices are derived from the reference scenario of the "World Energy Outlook, 2009 Edition" published by the International Energy Agency (IEA) in November 2009.

Based on the mentioned input data the estimation of the future trends in CO_2 emissions is derived. The diagram in Figure 8 shows the change in CO_2 emissions in the region by 2030, taking into account the variation of the mentioned parameters and assuming that there is no renewable energy activities and energy conservation actions have been implemented in the municipality ("do nothing" scenario). For Amyntaio municipality a gradual increase of CO_2 emissions is observed (0.13% by 2020 and 1.26% by 2020).

The criteria values of each alternative scenario are presented in Table 1.

Feasible Scenarios of Actions

Using the aspiration level for the criterion of CO_2 emissions reduction, namely 20% reduction by 2020, the scenarios S14, S15, S18, S19, S22, S23, S26, S27, S30, S31 and S32 are out from the evaluation process. These scenarios are illustrated with red points in Figure 9.

Value Function of Each Criterion

Following the decision maker's responses regarding the preferences, the development of marginal value factions (polynomial functions) is made (Figures 10 and 11).

Figure 8. Development of CO_2 emissions in the municipalities

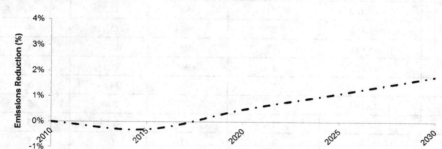

Table 1. Criteria values

Scenario	g_1	g_2	g_3	g_4	g_5
	Investment Cost for the Municipality (€)	Contribution to Employment (1-5)	Social Cost (€/resident)	CO_2 Emissions Reduction (%)	Effects on Natural Environment (1-5)
S1	98.608.467	5	989	40,73	1
S2	90.317.283	5	403	26,02	1
S3	87.516.632	3	403	25,77	1
S4	89.115.938	4	806	34,47	1
S5	96.223.873	5	947	36,97	1
S6	88.030.647	5	385	23,35	1
S7	85.229.996	3	385	23,10	1
S8	86.759.332	4	771	31,02	1
S9	77.374.934	5	989	36,53	2
S10	74.155.600	4	345	21,22	2
S11	65.705.600	3	345	21,80	2
S12	67.882.405	4	806	30,27	2
S13	75.158.267	4	989	34,64	2
S14	62.867.083	4	365	19,93	2
S15	64.066.432	3	403	19,68	2
S16	65.665.738	4	806	28,37	2
S17	22.373.073	3	989	27,66	2
S18	14.179.847	3	347	16,01	2
S19	11.379.196	2	385	15,76	2
S20	12.908.532	2	771	23,68	2
S21	20.324.334	3	991	29,61	3
S22	12.033.150	2	365	14,90	3
S23	9.232.499	2	403	14,65	3
S24	10.831.805	2	806	23,35	3
S25	18.107.667	2	989	27,72	4
S26	9.816.483	2	365	13,01	4
S27	7.015.832	1	403	12,76	4
S28	8.615.138	2	806	21,45	4
S29	14.450.504	2	976	28,84	5
S30	5.313.180	1	347	8,44	5
S31	2.512.529	1	385	8,19	5
S32	4.041.866	1	771	16,11	5

Figure 9. Aspiration level - CO_2 emissions reduction 20%

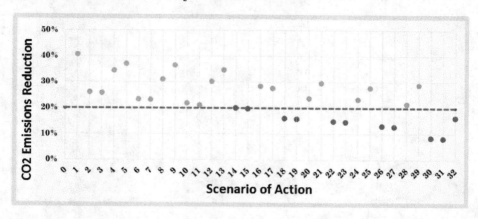

Figure 10. Decision maker's responses

Criteria Values (Qualitative X% / Quantitative)	Criteria values in order to generate marginal value factions				
	Criterion 1	Criterion 2	Criterion 3	Criterion 4	Criterion 5
0% / 1	0	0	0	0	0
20% / 2	0.48	0.21	0.18	0.44	0.72
40% / 3	0.72	0.78	0.38	0.76	0.81
60% / 4	0.85	0.92	0.65	0.95	0.86
80% / -	0.95		0.8	0.99	
100% / 5	1	1	1	1	1

Weights of the Criteria

The reference set of scenarios and the last column the decision maker's ranking are presented in Table 2.

Based on Table 2, a linear program according to (8) is formulated, with δ = 0.001. The linear program has multiple optimal solutions, since $[\min]F = \sum_{a \in A_R} \sigma^+(a) + \sigma^-(a) = 0$. Thus, in the post-optimality analysis, the algorithm searches for more characteristic solutions, which maximize the weights of each criterion. The average of five solutions is calculated (p_1 = 0,299, p_2 = 0,168, p_3 = 0,339, p_4 = 0,123, p_5 = 0,071). This solution corresponds to the marginal value functions and produces a ranking which is consistent with the decision maker's initial weak order (Table 3).

Figure 11. Value function of each criterion

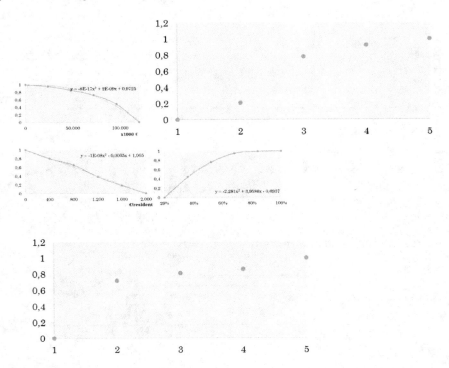

Table 2. Reference scenarios and ranking of the decision maker

Scenarios	g_1	g_2	g_3	g_4	g_5	Preference Order	Global Value
	Investment Cost for the Municipality	Contribution to Employment	Social Cost	CO_2 Emissions Reduction	Effects on Natural Environment		
A	0,81	0,92	0,66	0,26	0,72	1	0,026
B	0,97	0,78	0,51	0,26	0,72	2	0,000
C	0,97	0,78	0,59	0,01	0,81	2	0,089
D	0,99	0,21	0,59	0,01	0,81	4	0,000
E	0,62	0,78	0,63	0,01	0,81	4	0,039
F	0,62	0,78	0,51	0,07	0,72	6	0,021
G	0,39	0,92	0,51	0,26	0,72	7	0,026

Figure 12. Weights

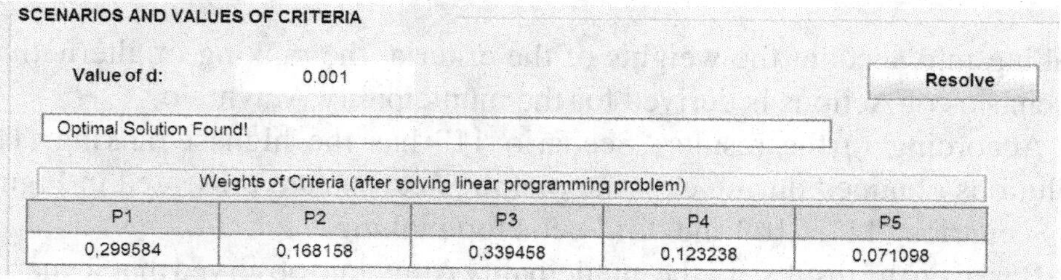

SCENARIOS AND VALUES OF CRITERIA

Value of d: 0.001   Resolve

Optimal Solution Found!

Weights of Criteria (after solving linear programming problem)

P1	P2	P3	P4	P5
0,299584	0,168158	0,339458	0,123238	0.071098

Table 3. Ranking: Multicriteria ordinal regression approach

No.	Value	Scenario
1	0,701	S11
2	0,698	S10
3	0,691	S21
4	0,678	S17
5	0,669	S12
5	0,669	S16
7	0,642	S9
8	0,630	S13
9	0,614	S6
10	0,612	S2
11	0,608	S20
12	0,607	S24
13	0,586	S7
14	0,584	S3
15	0,566	S8
16	0,561	S4
17	0,529	S5
18	0,522	S1

Ranking

Taking into account the weights of the criteria, the ranking of alternatives Scenarios of Actions is derived for the municipality Amyntaio.

According to the results "Scenario 11" has the highest ranking. The solutions obtained during extreme ranking analysis are presented in Figure 7. Scenarios "11", "10" and "21" get a top ranking.

Based on the results, for the municipality Amyntaio observed that scenarios that include the promotion of district heating projects and general local production of energy for heating / cooling are high in the ranking list, (S11 and S10 are in the first places). This is due to the geographical position of the municipality as well as the climatic conditions do favor the implementation of such projects, as in Amyntaio. Moreover, it was noted that Scenarios in which the participation of all sectors is very high, indicate very low yields, mainly because of very high costs required for their implementation, both on the part of the municipality and from the part of citizens.

From the robustness analysis can also be observed that the differences between the extreme positions of alternatives Scenarios are sometimes lower and sometimes higher. In particular, greater deviations are detected in S8 Scenarios for Amyntaio. In general, the final ranking for the Municipality of Amyntaio is quite stable (average range ranking positions 2,8).

The local government's reform through "Kallikrates" decentralized operational plan has created all the conditions for a development model based

Figure 13. Extreme ranking positions of alternative scenarios

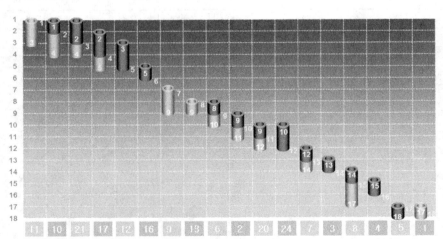

largely on local authorities. The Municipality of Amyntaio already possesses several of the necessary conditions to exploit development opportunities, to undertake the coordination role among the local actors and to implement a central strategy within its regulatory role in the local development.

Final Decision

Table 4 shows the efficiency index of the Scenarios of Actions "S11", "S10" and "S21".

Finally, the local community selects "Scenario 11" (Table 5) for its SEAP, submitted in September 2013 (Amyntaio, 2013).

The overall CO_2 emission reduction target by 2020 is 21,8%. In this context, the municipality has committed to implement a series of appropriate renewable energy and rational use of energy activities in its territory, laying balanced emphasis on the local energy and heat production, and the promotion and implementation of measures on energy savings. Indeed, the area's univocal

Table 4. Efficiency index

	S11	S10	S21
Efficiency Index	1,52	1,28	1,38
Total Value	0,701	0,698	0,691
Ranking	1-3	1-4	1-4

Table 5. Description of "S11"

Sector	Expected Energy Savings/ Production (MWh)	Expected CO_2 Emission Reduction (tn CO_2)	Cost (€)
Agriculture	5.486,3	3.906,5	636.000
Municipal sector	1.339,7	1.122,4	3.447.000
Residential sector	9.858,1	4.290,6	96.000
Tertiary sector	2.688,5	2.035,4	52.000
Public lighting	554,6	633,9	700.000
Transport	10.742,5	3.433,8	1.914.000
Local electricity produced	3.511,9	4.840,8	1.810.000
Local heating/cooling produced	46.215,7	9.826,3	57.050.600
Total	80.397,3	30.089,8	65.705.600

economy orientation of energy production through lignite is considered as a basic, inhibitory factor towards sustainability. A significant part of the CO_2 emissions' reduction will come from the installation of biomass district heating systems in local communities.

The overall estimated budget for the elaboration of the foreseen actions is 65.705.600 €. It should be noted that, a part of the estimated budget will come from external sources, such as European, national or regional funding schemes. In this context, the Municipality of Amyntaio has already focused its efforts on the participation in relevant funding programmes and initiatives, such as the Action Plan "ENERGOPOLIS", the programme "EKSIKONOMO" and the Operational Programme under the National Strategic Reference Framework (NSRF).

PHASE III: MONITORING

Targets

The last stage of the methodology consists of the monitoring and evaluation of the Action Plan, through the Methodological Approach for Monitoring SEC Targets. The targets of each evaluation indicator for each activity sector are presented in the Table 6 (according to the defined categories, namely "Energy", "Environment", "Economy" and "Infrastructure & Information").

Implementation Progress of Actions and Measures

The evaluation year of the Action Plan is 2013. The progress achieved in regards to the implementation of the actions and measures for each activity sector is presented below:

- **Agricultural Sector:** Establishment of agricultural development department, aiming to technologically support and continually inform farmers about the available funding programmes. However, little progress has been achieved in regards to the modernization of farming tractors and irrigation techniques;
- **Municipal Buildings, Equipment/Facilities:** Energy upgrade of specific municipal buildings;

Table 6. Targets for each sector

Symbol	Agriculture	Municipal Buildings, Equipment/ Facilities	Residential Sector	Tertiary Sector	Outdoor Lighting	Public/ Municipal Transports	Private/ Commercial Transports
I_1	Energy						
I_{11}	3,34	0,61	7,84	1,76	0,11	0,14	4,26
I_{12}	1,26	0,25	1,14	0,89	0,11	0,00	0,00
I_{13}	2,09	0,26	4,90	0,43	0,00	0,14	4,26
I_2	Environment						
I_{21}	1,97	0,36	3,07	1,31	0,12	0,02	1,09
I_{22}	0,59	0,61	0,39	0,74	1,08	0,12	0,25
I_{23}	0,00	0,20	1,18	1,10	0,01	0,00	0,00
I_3	Economy						
I_{31}	4,28	195,28	265,36	72,46	8,18	7,61	2,15
I_{32}	0,85	105,86	155,77	14,20	3,88	2,46	0,15
I_4	Infrastructure and Information						
I_{41}	0,00	0,25	0,12	0,01	1,15	0,00	0,00
I_{42}	1,25	6,87	1,16	1,16	-	5,89	2,26

I_{11} Energy consumption per capita (MWh/capita)
I_{12} Electricity use in final energy consumption (MWh/capita)
I_{13} Fossil fuel use in final energy consumption (MWh/capita)
I_{21} CO_2 emissions per capita (tnCO_2/capita)
I_{22} CO_2 emission intensity index (tnCO_2/MWh)
I_{23} Use of renewable energy sources (MWh/capita)
I_{31} Total budget spent (€/capita)
I_{32} Funding from external sources (€/capita)
I_{41} Integration level of automations, smart meters and ICT (%)
I_{42} Level of awareness (%)

- **Residential Sector:** Given the fact that the local authority does not have the capability to immediately influence the energy end-users of the household sector, focus has been given on the citizens' information and awareness;
- **Tertiary Sector:** Information and awareness of the professionals of the tertiary sector, in order to reduce final consumption and the respective CO_2 emissions;
- **Municipal Lighting:** Progress has been achieved in replacing existing lamps with new, more efficient ones;
- **Transport:** Progress has been achieved, with emphasis given on the increase of use of public transport and the more efficient management of the municipal fleet;

- **Local Electrical Energy Production:** During the period 2009-2013 most actions for local electrical energy production involved the installation of photovoltaic systems;
- **Local Heating/Cooling Production:** The municipality focuses on the extension of the district heating infrastructure.

Values of the Monitoring Indicators for the Evaluation Year

Taking into consideration the Baseline Emission Inventory for the evaluation year 2014, as well as the implementation progress of the suggested actions and measures, the values of the evaluation indicators for each activity sector of the municipality are calculated (Table 7); the distance of each evaluation

Table 7. Values of the monitoring indicators for the evaluation year

Symbol	Agriculture	Municipal Buildings, Equipment/ Facilities	Residential Sector	Tertiary Sector	Public Lighting	Public/ Municipal Transports	Private/ Commercial Transports
I_1	Energy						
I_{11}	16,00	26,39	12,00	5,43	38,84	8,93	6,53
I_{12}	12,16	24,63	13,45	6,80	38,84	0,00	0,00
I_{13}	19,50	18,45	11,07	8,15	-	6,96	5,99
I_2	Environment						
I_{21}	18,05	24,87	10,67	6,79	33,66	9,14	5,18
I_{22}	6,12	16,10	19,04	10,69	23,52	1,99	10,59
I_{23}	0,10	22,21	13,05	14,80	38,35	9,69	0,54
I_3	Economy						
I_{31}	11,37	18,25	13,96	9,97	19,74	8,95	7,59
I_{32}	4,51	24,73	13,66	5,58	20,80	4,45	3,53
I_4	Infrastructure and Information						
I_{41}	0,00	1,67	0,60	0,07	2,88	0,00	0,00
I_{42}	5,00	8,59	3,31	4,64	-	7,36	6,46

I_{11} Energy consumption per capita (MWh/capita)
I_{12} Electricity use in final energy consumption (MWh/capita)
I_{13} Fossil fuel use in final energy consumption (MWh/capita)
I_{21} CO_2 emissions per capita (tnCO_2/capita)
I_{22} CO_2 emission intensity index (tnCO_2/MWh)
I_{23} Use of renewable energy sources (MWh/capita)
I_{31} Total budget spent (€/capita)
I_{32} Funding from external sources (€/capita)
I_{41} Integration level of automations, smart meters and ICT (%)
I_{42} Level of awareness (%)

indicator is calculated from the target set, using the "proximity-to-target" approach.

Calculation of the "SEC$_{Index}$"

Based on the methodology presented in the second Chapter, the progress in each category (Energy, Environment, Economy, Infrastructure and Information) is presented in Table 8.

The "SEC$_{Index}$" is calculated, presenting the progress that has been achieved in each activity sector and the whole municipality, in regards to the accomplishment of the targets set during the development of the Action Plan (Figures 14 and 15).

Table 8. Results

Symbol	Energy	Environment	Economy	Infrastructure and Information	"SEC$_{Index}$"
Agriculture	5,1%	2,9%	1,5%	0,4%	9,9%
Municipal buildings, equipment/facilities	7,5%	7,4%	4,1%	0,8%	19,8%
Residential sector	3,9%	4,9%	2,6%	0,3%	11,8%
Tertiary sector	2,1%	3,8%	1,5%	0,4%	7,8%
Outdoor lighting	12,4%	11,2%	3,9%	0,2%	27,7%
Public/municipal transports	1,8%	2,5%	1,3%	0,6%	6,2%
Private/commercial transports	1,4%	1,8%	1,1%	0,5%	4,9%

Figure 14. Depiction of results in each activity sector

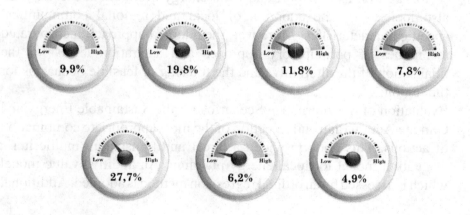

Figure 15. Index "SECIndex" of Amyntaio municipality

DISCUSSION

The proposed "MPC⁺" approach and the relevant "Action³" information system developed, can support the local authorities to the:

- Development of the alternative Scenarios of Actions, namely a set of energy actions and interventions, taking into consideration the specific characteristics of the region. An initial design of alternative Scenarios took place according to a knowledge-based process. In this respect, a number of renewable energy and rational use of energy actions were identified for the agricultural, public, tertiary and residential sector, as well as transport and local energy production. Efforts were also focused on the adoption of local and regional communities' specific characteristics. Moreover, the adopted approach incorporated techniques of participatory approach and aspiration levels for the finalisation of the alternative and the filtering of feasible Scenarios for the region;
- Evaluation of the alternative Scenarios for the Sustainable Energy and Climate Action Plan and selection of the most appropriate combination of actions. This book provided a direct and transparent multicriteria evaluation model for local energy planning. An additive value model which is assessed by an ordinal regression method is adopted. Additional

algorithms were incorporated using extreme ranking analysis, in order to identify multiple optimal solutions.

Further issues for the extension of the previous research is that different techniques could be incorporated to support the construction of the criteria value functions. More specifically, the construction of the value functions could be based on the use of functions with the general form $u = u(a,b,c;g_i)$. These general forms of functions are able to generate a satisfactory set of value functions of the criterion g_i for the different values of the parameters a, b and c. Moreover, visual procedures could be included, in order to provide a user-friendly environment.

CONCLUSION

The pilot application of the MPC[+] approach (through the support of the information system developed) in real problem, provided the possibility to evaluate its completeness and the results' reliability. The proposed approach provides a direct and clear definition of all the problem aspects and thorough analysis of the interactions between them in the process of design and evaluation of the alternative Scenarios of Actions by decision makers.

What differentiates the use of the information system "Action[3]", which incorporates the proposed MPC[+] approach, from other similar efforts is summarized at the following five points:

- The multi-criteria analysis and robustness analysis, supporting the decision-making process of the local authorities;
- The agricultural sector is studied separately due to its especially high energy consumptions in rural areas. At the final stage is being embodied to the tertiary sector consumption, according to the guidelines;
- The user is provided with different methodological approaches in the specification of the energy consumptions when a lack of data at the municipal level is concerned;
- The existence of a detailed database of renewable energy and rational use of energy best practices;
- A monitoring module, monitoring potential deviations based either on energy consumption, or on activity data.

An important element of the procedure for the assessment of the methodology was the direct communication with the local authorities and other stakeholders, as well as the availability of real data and reliable information within the framework of the European project "eReNet - Rural Web Energy Learning Network for Action" and particularly during the development of the Sustainable Energy and Climate Action Plans of the selected municipality.

ACKNOWLEDGMENT

A part of the current chapter was based on the relevant activities conducted within the framework of the project "Rural Web Energy Learning Network for Action – eReNet (Project no: IEE/10/224/SI2.593412), supported by the Intelligent Energy – Europe (IEE) Programme. The content of the chapter is the sole responsibility of its author and does not necessary reflect the views of the EC.

REFERENCES

Amyntaio. (2013). *Sustainable Energy Action Plan of the Municipality of Amyntaio*. Retrieved December 16, 2015, from: http://www.covenantofmayors.eu/about/signatories_en.html?city_id=4310&seap

Hellenic Statistical Authority. (2015). Retrieved December 16, 2015, from: http://www.statistics.gr/en/home/

Chapter 5
Building Future "Smart Energy Cities":
The Role of ICT and IoT Solutions

ABSTRACT

In the process of building the future cities, Information and Communication Technology (ICT) and Internet of Things (IoT) solutions are the key enablers. Although there are plenty of energy related data available in the cities, there are no established methodologies and validated tools to collect, integrate and analyse them so that they can support energy use optimization. In this context, the aim of this chapter is to present the Smart Cities IoT Platform. A "wireless telemetry cloud" over the city can be created, which facilitates the transferring of open data from the distributed sources (weather station, installed equipment, etc.). The proposed IoT Platform is composed of prediction models, scenarios and rules, as well as a database to store the data and results. With the Smart Cities IoT Platform, web-based applications can be created, customised to the specific characteristics and needs of end-users, including the fields of buildings, infrastructure, transport, generation and storage.

DOI: 10.4018/978-1-5225-2286-7.ch005

INTRODUCTION

Smart Energy Cities, as a core pillar of the Smart Cities, constitute an emerging urban development strategy and are expected to play a key role in the implementation of Europe 2020. Among the primary targets of Smart Energy Cities is also the achievement of the 2030 climate and energy objectives, towards carbon neutral cities and neighbourhoods (Doukas et al., 2017). In the process of building the future Cities, Information and Communication Technology (ICT) and Internet of Things (IoT) solutions are the key enablers.

Although there are plenty of energy related data available in the cities, there are no established methodologies and validated tools to collect, integrate and analyse them so that they can support energy use optimization (Androulaki et al., 2016). Until now, we have witnessed only sporadic and ad hoc efforts in this multidisciplinary scientific field. An intelligent and integrated assessment and consideration of various data sets, as well as relevant intelligent systems in a transparent and accessible manner is required.

Monitoring and optimization of available energy sources are expected to be the key factors contributing to market growth. However, it is of common understanding that achieving energy savings at a city level is a difficult and complex process. In this respect, modelling and simulation are invaluable to better understand how cities work and how the various different domains interact among them, such as energy demand, renewable energy systems and innovative generation technologies for local energy production, energy and data infrastructures, etc. Models and datasets, however, typically cover one particular field only and it is difficult to connect them across these boundaries. When incorporating (real-time) data in the models or using external open datasets as input, new challenges arise on interpretation, extrapolation and interpolation in addition to access constraints due to specific domain boundaries and processes.

In this context, the aim of this Chapter is to present the Smart Cities IoT Platform. A "wireless telemetry cloud" over the city can be created, which facilitates the transferring of open data from the distributed sources (weather station, installed equipment, etc.). The proposed IoT Platform is composed of prediction models, scenarios and rules, as well as a database to store the data and results. With the Smart Cities IoT Platform, web-based applications can be created, customised to the specific characteristics and needs of end-users, including the fields of buildings, infrastructure, transport, generation and storage.

Apart from the introduction, the paper is structured along four sections. Section 2 provides the current trends in Smart Cities and their main components, namely Smart Grids and microgrids, driverless cars, automated buildings and advanced sensors. Section 3 presents initiatives from the international literature, related to the ideas of optimizing the energy use in cities. The Smart Cities IoT Platform is introduced in Section 3. Two innovative ICT solutions are presented in Section 4, namely the web-based DSS and the integrated Web Portal. Finally, the last section is summarizing the key issues that have arisen in this paper.

CURRENT TRENDS IN SMART CITIES

The operation of Smart Cities is grounded on the utilization of ICT technologies, leading to a reduction of energy consumption, waste and other resources, and a greater quality of life via enhanced residents' engagement. ICT solutions and IoT are essential to implement smart energy systems (Dassani et al., 2015). ICT solutions, Internet of Things IoT and Data Analytics are essential to implement smart energy systems; in fact they drive models and methods for planning and operation of future integrated energy platforms. According to Navigant Research, the global market for smart energy solutions is expected to grow from $7.3 billion (annual revenue) in 2015 to $21 billion by 2024, representing a cumulative investment of almost $140 billion (Woods, 2016).

Nowadays, there are strong governmental programs for extended smart energy deployment, while a number of Smart Cities projects exist already and numerous new smart energy city initiatives are planned for the near future. Spain, United Arab Emirates (UAE), Singapore and Australia, across the world governments and companies are investing heavily in smart city research and projects (Lima, 2016). The Catalonian capital, Barcelona, is rapidly becoming a smart metropolis and a world tech capital. Government-deployed sensors will collect and coordinate an unprecedented amount of data on daily life in the Singapore city (Watts & Purnell, 2016). The Dubai Smart City initiative aims to transform the emirate into a leading global Smart City over the next few years. The strategy includes over 100 initiatives and a plan to transform 1000 government services into smart services. According to Cisco, Dubai's public and private sector IT market is valued at $4.87 bn over the next five years, including a public sector opportunity of $1.17 bn (Kwang, 2016). In Abu Dhabi, the Masdar City aims to be the world's first sustainable "Smart City" with no carbon footprint. Masdar City is proof that a clean city is no longer a utopian vision but a genuine urban model that substantially reduces greenhouse-gas emissions. The concept has already inspired other cities to take action, including Vancouver, Nantes, Lyon and Stockholm (Smith & Gordon, 2017).

Rapid expansion of city borders, driven by increase in population and infrastructure development, would force city borders to expand outward and engulf the surrounding daughter cities to form mega cities, each with a population of more than 10 million (Frost & Sullivan, 2017).

The technological components of a Smart City include among others Smart Grids and microgrids, driverless cars, automated buildings and advanced sensors. A short description of these components is provided in the following paragraphs.

Smart Grids

The general connectivity in the energy system, made possible by ICT platforms, creates a two-way flow of information, connecting all components, assets and other hardware in the system, in order to allow the development of efficient, reliable and decentralized Smart Grids. According to Global e-Sustainability Initiative, the evolution of Smart Grids could create $2.1 billion in additional revenues for the ICT sector (GeSI, 2015). It is estimated that Gulf Cooperation Council (GCC) countries can save up to USD 10 billion in infrastructural investment by 2020 through the use of Smart Grid, which optimises supply and demand by using information technology to provide a two-way flow of real time information between power generation, grid operators and consumers (ME CONSTRUCION NEWS, 2017). As a consequence, the success of Smart Grids depends on the development of well-defined ICT solutions able to process big data and support decision making within a decentralized energy generation, storage and distribution system.

Microgrids

Microgrids represent a new concept for future energy distribution system. Their capability to operate independently can make microgrids a key driver for the adoption of Internet of Things technologies and the promotion of Smart Cities model (Power, 2016). Moreover, the integration of small-scale renewable energy resources into domestic households enables consumers to become producers of green energy. These households can collectively reduce their carbon footprint and dependence on fossil-fuelled power plants by trading locally produced renewable energy. Incentivizing the trade of green energy is a necessary step in order to boost the renewable economy (Mihaylov, 2015).

Bitcoin has been called "digital gold". Blockchain, the technology underlying bitcoin and other cryptocurrencies, is a digital ledger that enables peer-to-peer trading. A microgrid that use Blockchain technology to enable local energy trading is currently developing in Brooklyn. Brooklyn Microgrid (2017) aims to create a local, neighbourhood-powered grid that could operate in parallel to the main grid. It will allow rooftop photovoltaic systems to feed excess electricity back to the local grid and receive payments from the purchasers (Maloney, 2016). This project is the first version of a new kind of energy market, operated by consumers, which will change the way we generate and consume electricity (Rutkin, 2016).

Self-Driving Vehicles

We can envision a future where self-driving vehicles will be integrated in Smart Grids (Falleni, 2016). Autonomous driving can change the way we think about traffic. We can plan our drive with a mix of autonomous and active driving, making our journey more time-efficient. Goldman Sachs predicts North American auto sales could be almost 60% autonomous by 2030, divided between "limited self-driving" cars, which may require driver control during difficult conditions and "full self-driving" cars, which can drive alone in all situations (Grabar H., 2016).

Energy Management in Buildings

The energy sector is closely interconnected with the building sector and integrated ICT solutions for effective energy management supporting decision making at building, district and city level are key fundamental elements for making a city smart. Through the use of ICT-based management systems, the building's intelligent systems can communicate with the energy providers to control cooling, heating, lighting and hot water systems, to ensure a more stable energy supply, optimising the management of demand peaks and resources at a local level.

The international smart building market is expected to touch $36.3 billion by 2020 from $7.26 billion in 2015, growing at a compound annual growth rate of 38 per cent (Green, 2017). The connectivity and data flow associated with the IoT will support the broader adoption of Building Energy Management Systems.

Rich sources of data enable better ways to manage and measure buildings and portfolios of buildings. Big data captured by buildings can enable owners to deliver energy savings, make more efficient use of space, and provide tenants with commercially valuable insights that will justify higher rental income — and impact the potential returns investors can realise from commercial real estate. Considering that 90% of all data generated by devices like smartphones, connected meters and appliances is never analysed or acted upon, the ability to integrate intelligent devices for data analytics will be key to gain competitive advantage and meet the needs of an ever-growing audience of energy management stakeholders.

OPTIMIZING THE ENERGY USE IN CITIES

Several initiatives have been identified in the international research scene, relevant to the ideas of optimizing the energy use in cities:

- In terms of semantic data modelling –a modelling technique that enables information stored in different formats and different places to be used to create a multi-level energy model of an area -, the SEMANCO initiative (Semantic Tools for Carbon Reduction in Urban Planning) is worth mentioning. The technological approach of the project is based on the integration of energy related open data, structured according to standards, semantically modelled and interoperable with a set of tools for visualizing, simulating and analysing the multiple relationships between the factors determining CO_2 production. The tools and methods in SEMANCO enable structuring energy related data, held in distributed sources and diverse formats, using data mining techniques (SEMANCO Project Methodology Report, 2012);
- The CitInES initiative (Design of a decision support tool for sustainable, reliable and cost-effective energy strategies in cities and industrial complexes) aims to design innovative energy system modelling and optimization algorithms to allow end-users to optimize their energy strategy using data sources on local energy generation, storage, transport, distribution and demand, including demand-side management and functionalities enabled by smart grid technologies. CitInES integrates information about local renewable energies, smart

grid integration and demand-side management, as well as fuel price uncertainties (Page et. al., 2013);

- The ICT 4 E2B FORUM (European stakeholders forum crossing value and innovation chains to explore needs, challenges and opportunities in further research and integration of ICT systems for Energy Efficiency in Buildings) aims to the creation of a strategic research roadmap for ICT supported energy efficiency in construction, by bringing together all relevant stakeholders involved in ICT systems and solutions for energy efficiency in buildings, at identifying and reviewing the needs in terms of research and systems integration as well as at accelerating implementation and take-up (Mastrodonato et. al., 2011);

- In the framework of IREEN (ICT Roadmap for Energy Efficient Neighbourhoods) initiative the ways that ICT for energy efficiency and performance can be extended beyond individual homes and buildings to the wider context of neighbourhoods and communities are examined;

- NiCE (Networking intelligent Cities for Energy Efficiency) promotes the implementation of commitments to the Green Digital Charter while in the framework of FINSENY (Future Internet for Smart Energy) initiative Future Internet technologies are exploited for the development of Smart Energy infrastructures, enabling new functionality while reducing costs (Fluhr & Williams, 2011);

- ENPROVE (Energy consumption prediction with building usage measurements for software-based decision support) provides an innovative service to model the energy consumption of structures supported by sensor-based data. The service makes use of novel ICT solutions to predict the performance of alternative energy-savings building scenarios in order to support relevant stakeholders in the procedure of identifying optimal investments for maximizing energy efficiency of an existing building;

- The INTENSE initiative (From Estonia till Croatia: Intelligent Energy Saving Measures for Municipal housing in Central and Eastern European countries) provides a holistic approach for planning of energy optimized housing. The project comprises an analysis of legal preconditions, experience exchange on best practice examples, pilot planning activities at partner municipalities, and public awareness raising;

- i-SCOPE (Interoperable Smart City services through an Open Platform for urban Ecosystems) delivers an open platform on top of which it develops, within different domains, a series of "smart city" services, based on interoperable 3D Urban Information Models (UIMs) (Patti et. al., 2013);

- In the framework of RESSOL-MEDBUILD (RESearch Elevation on Integration of SOLar Technologies into MEDiterranean BUILDings) simulation models are developed for the optimization of building energy management and energy performance (RESSOL-MEDBUILD Periodic Report Summary, 2013);

- The ENRIMA initiative (Energy Efficiency and Risk Management in Public Buildings) specifies the development of a DSS engine for integrated management of energy-efficient sites, promoting adaptation of the DSS on buildings and/or spaces of public use (Cano et. al., 2013);

- TRACE (Tool for Rapid Assessment of City Energy) is a DSS tool designed and implemented by World Bank within the Energy Sector Management Assistance Program (ESMAP) to assist municipal authorities in identifying and prioritizing Energy Efficiency actions. The methodology incorporated within the TRACE project initially evaluates the city performance focusing on energy consuming municipal sectors (passenger transport, municipal buildings, water and wastewater, public lighting, power and heat, and solid waste), and then it prioritizes energy efficiency improvement actions and interventions for the most energy intense sectors (ESMAP WorldBank, 2010).

Optimizing the energy use in cities is a current research trend, with several existing initiatives promoting the use of DSSs in local communities' energy planning. Although many research initiatives have been proposed so far, there is a gap in integrating data from multiple domains (e.g. weather forecasts, occupants' feedback, energy prices, energy profiles), with the use of semantic technologies, to assist city authorities to produce short-term energy plans in a transparent and comprehensive way. Modelling and simulation are valuable tools to understand how cities work and how the various different elements interact among them (Doyle, 2009), such as renewable energy systems and innovative generation technologies for local energy production, as well as smart electricity grids and smart district heating/cooling grids. Models and datasets, however, typically cover one particular field only and it is difficult to span across its boundaries.

Except from the usually considered data sources that are focusing on energy, there are also other types of data, which may affect the energy demand and energy production at the city level, such as weather conditions and data on events that can affect energy use and patterns. To this end, a considerable variety of data sources need to be used to fully reflect the most important aspects that affect the energy use in a city on the one side, as well as to take into consideration the most important parameters in the decision-making process.

SMART CITIES IOT PLATFORM

This section presents the innovative "Smart Cities IoT Platform" (Figure 1). The proposed platform sits on the top of existing management systems, integrating data sources from various domains (storage, generation, transport, infrastructure and buildings). A "wireless telemetry cloud" over the city can be created, which facilitates the transferring of open data from the distributed

Figure 1. "Smart Cities IoT Platform"

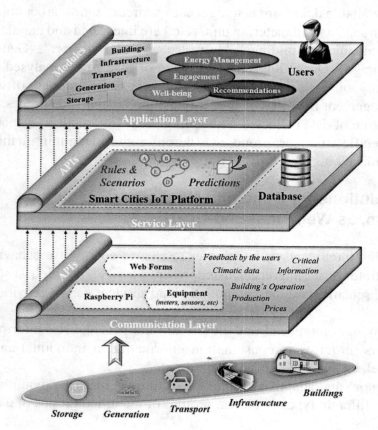

sources (Communication Layer). The proposed IoT Platform is composed of prediction models, scenarios and rules, as well as a database to store the data and results (Service Layer). Web-based applications, customised to the specific characteristics and needs of the end users, can be provided (Application Layer).

Energy Management Services and Energy Use Optimization

Energy management services can be provided to the local authorities through the "Smart Cities IoT Platform". The purpose is to optimize the energy use in main city's buildings (municipal and educational buildings, buildings for entertainment and sports facilities, hospitals, hotels, etc.), taking into consideration their interaction with energy systems, such as renewable energy production, smart district heating and cooling grids through CHP (Combined Heat and Power) and other energy sources.

The available data from heterogeneous sources (e.g. weather conditions, data from sensors and metering units, etc.) are integrated and handled by the relevant modules: "Buildings", "Infrastructure", "Transport", "Generation" and "Storage". Depending on the volume of data to be analysed and the complexity of analysis, the Web Portal integrates suitable software for the management of different user groups, the content, the processing and presentation of data collected. Integrating prediction models, scenarios and rules, specific actions are proposed to the city authorities aiming at the energy use optimisation.

ICT Solutions for Buildings Managers, Buildings Owners, as Well Final End-Users

Integrating intelligent methodologies to change energy use behaviour and demonstrate causal inferences using, where possible, the highest standards of social scientific validation, the following services can be provided:

- Easy-to-comprehend and close real-time personalized information to users, in terms of consumption information at individual and group level, energy saving leader boards, etc.;
- Custom and adaptive incentive structures to meet the requirements of the different types of human profiles of identified groups of users;

- Analytical tailor-made recommendations, so as to enhance energy efficiency by behavioural change of users, making informed decisions;
- Provision of two interactive services to the users, namely thermal comfort validation and security, having a positive impact in health and safety.

In this context, innovative technological solutions for the local authorities (web-based Decision Support System and integrated Web Portal) that assist them to optimize the energy use in their premises and reduce CO_2 emissions are presented in the following Section.

DECISION SUPPORT TOOLS

Web-Based Decision Support System (DSS)

The proposed DSS relies on the integration of heterogeneous data sources using Semantic Web technologies, in order to suggest short-term Actions Plans for public authorities with the goal of reducing energy consumption. It has been developed within the framework of the project financed by the European Commission, titled "OPTIMising the energy USe in cities with smart decision support systems (OPTIMUS)".

Based on real-time data monitored (weather conditions, buildings' energy profiles, feedback provided by occupants, energy prices and energy production) and predicted data produced by the prediction models, DSS (OPTIMUS, 2014) introduces a list of practical Action Plans (Figure 2). A total of seven Action Plans, are available from the DSS, ready to accommodate energy managers willing to plug - in their buildings. The Action Plans refer to the energy optimization in buildings, examining them not as isolated entities. Taking into consideration their interaction with energy systems, they can foster efficient management of energy flows at a broader level, integrating energy demand, generation and data/energy infrastructures. DSS is characterized by a combination of advanced technologies that enables integration of multiple domains. The action plans are categorized, according to their applicability, to buildings and/or block of buildings, with some of them allowing more comfort, functionality, and flexibility through integration of energy generation and storage systems ("Sustainable Districts & Built Environment" Domain). Moreover, some of the action plans enable the interconnection of energy

Figure 2. OPTIMUS DSS

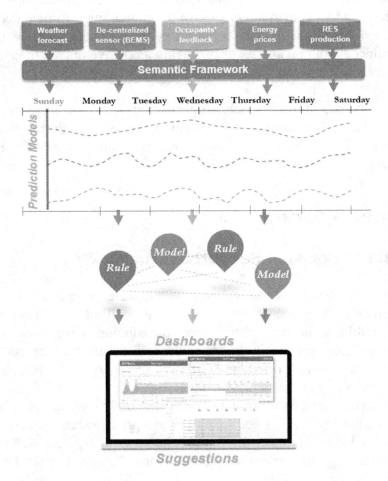

infrastructures and new technologies ("Integrated Infrastructures & Processes across Energy and ICT" Domain).

Table 1 provides the expected range of each action plan's impact on different aspects of energy optimization. The full potential is estimated from each action plan, both empirically and through literature. The numbers presented in Table 1 have been duly assessed and considered reliable for the purposes of the analysis.

The effectiveness of the OPTIMUS DSS has been verified through a substantial validation phase in the Savona Campus (20.690 m^2) and Savona "Colombo-Pertini School" (6.092 m^2) in Italy, among others. In the two pilot sites, the natural gas consumption is mainly related to the heating

Table 1. Potential impact of the action plans

Action Plan		Use	MIN	MAX	Reference
Reduction of Energy Consumption					
AP1	Scheduling and management of the occupancy	Cooling	5%	9%	"The results showed that room reassignment could further enhance the energy use reduction by up to 4,4% for heating and 9% for cooling" (Yang and Becerik-Gerber, 2014) "~8-11% energy savings" (UNC, 2016)
		Heating	2%	4%	
AP2	Scheduling the set-point temperature	Cooling	5%	9%	"For each degree rise in supply-air temperature set point, there is about 5% to 6% reduction in total HVAC energy consumption, depending on climate", (Fernandez et al., 2012) "A reduction of 1 K in internal temperature will reduce the energy consumption by 6%" (Sala et al., 1999). "Energy savings using an adaptive comfort model was estimated as 10 ÷ 18% of the overall cooling load" (Attia and Carlucci, 2015).
		Heating	5%	9%	
AP3	Scheduling the ON/OFF of the heating system	Heating	5%	10%	"The replacement of existing fixed start time control with optimum start/stop control can generate 10% energy savings for heating systems operating single shifts (Curbontrust, 2016).
AP4	Management of the air side economizer	Cooling	10%	20%	"As much as 20% savings in electrical energy for cooling were possible with demand-controlled ventilation" (Brandemuehl and Braun, 1999). "Comfort is largely enhanced without mechanical cooling and reaches usual criteria while impact on energy demand is limited to 10% of heating demand (Moeseke et al., 2007).
		Heating	5%	10%	
Increase of RES Production					
AP5	Scheduling the photovoltaic (PV) maintenance		3%	8%	Empirically (based on the available data from the pilot cities)
Reduction of Energy Cost					
AP6	Scheduling the sale/ consumption of the electricity produced through the PV system		5%	10%	"The cost savings achieved by charging according to the price-optimal strategy was about 10-15%" (Steen et al., 2016). "research shows that 20%–30% of building energy consumption can be saved through optimized operation and management without changing the structure and hardware configuration of the building energy supply system." (Guan, 2010). "Energy costs with and without battery" (reductions between 7 and 10%) (Guan, 2010)
AP7	Scheduling the operation of heating and electricity systems towards energy cost optimization		5%	10%	

needs, while electricity consumption is mainly related to the cooling, DHW, lighting, etc. A microgrid has been installed in Savona Campus, including PV system, energy storage equipment (battery), as well as two Cogeneration Heat and Power System (CHP) units. PV systems have been also installed in the "Colombo-Pertini School". During the baseline year, the total electricity consumption was estimated at 900 MWh/year in the Campus and 42 MWh/year in the School, the total natural gas at 1.361[1] MWh/year in the Campus and 582 MWh/year in the School and the energy production at 668 MWh/year in the Campus and 20 MWh/year in the School.

The results from the OPTIMUS DSS pilot operation are summarized below (Capozzoli et al., 2016):

- **Savona Campus:** The application of the AP5 increases the renewable energy produced of 7%. The AP7 reduces the CO_2 emission of 4% and the energy cost of 3%, while increases the renewable energy produced of 6%;

- **Savona "Colombo-Pertini School":** The AP2 according to adaptive comfort model can reduce the annual delivered natural gas for space heating (and consequently of CO_2 emission and energy cost) of 4%. This reduction is due to the decreasing of the set point temperature for the entire heating season (from October to April) of 0,5°C. Only 1% of reduction has been evaluated for the application of the AP3. This is due to the fact that the management of the heating system is already performed through an algorithm aimed at optimizing the boost time. An average increasing of renewable energy produced of 8% have been calculated by applying the AP5. The loads shifting suggested by the AP6 decreases the CO_2 emission of 2,5%, decreases the energy cost of 2% and increases the renewable energy consumed of 2,5%.

Moreover, the following conclusions can be drawn for the two pilot sites, based on the results of the OPTIMUS SCEAF Tool (Papastamatiou et al., 2016) from the ex-ante (2014, baseline year) and ex-post (2016, evaluation year) application:

- The Savona Campus has slightly increased its performance in some of the SCEAF indicators leading to a higher total score. More specifically, the pilot scores a "Very Low+0.14" for the baseline year and a "Very

Low+0.48" for the year after the implementation of the DSS. It should be noted that the improvement inspected is negligible mainly due to the implementation of only two Action Plans, from which no-one directly reduces energy consumption. In particular, AP5 increases the production of energy leading indirectly to lower CO_2 emission levels. However, the PV production is minor compared to the electricity produced by the CHP systems or absorbed by the net, making it impossible for the AP to achieve any major improvements. The same stands for AP7 which, although it decreases energy cost and improves self-consumption through the optimization of CHP use, it does not significantly affect the amount of energy delivered and therefore the energy footprint of the campus;

- The Savona School has significantly increased its performance in the majority of the SCEAF indicators leading to a higher total score. More specifically, the pilot scores a "Very Low-0.04" (0.96) for the baseline year and a "Medium-0.33" (2.67) for the year after the implementation of the DSS. This means that the performance of the pilot in terms of energy optimization can be improved through the DSS by almost 2 classes. The results are reasonable given the reduction of the natural gas reported, as well as the installation of new monitoring and forecasting systems and the exploitation of the occupants' feedback towards energy optimization.

Integrated Web Portal

The proposed Web Portal aims to provide energy management services to the local authorities through a web-based platform. It has been developed within the framework of the project ESCO Smart City Energy Plan (ESCOCITY), co-financed by the General Secretariat for Research and Technology (GSRT) of the Hellenic Ministry of Culture, Education and Religious Affairs.

In order to be easily applicable and customizable, the platform has been implemented in a modular environment. The Portal's design is based on open source tools, so that no license fees are required for its implementation. The necessary equipment for the installation of the Web Portal consists of:

- Metering devices, which measure the energy data;
- The central gateway with an integrated OPC server, which collects the measured data by MODBUS protocol;

- The gateway manages and sends the data to the central MySQL database.

The platform integrates data analysis software, in order to calculate energy indicators by handling two types of data:

- Static data, related to the main characteristics of each element, e.g. a building's surface area, and change rarely. These data are inserted by authorized users though appropriate forms;
- Dynamic data that change with a frequency and are collected by the metering devices.

The core of the Data Analysis Tool is "Plotalot", which is used to make charts and graphs presenting the data collected, or the indicators which are calculated from them.

Depending on the volume of data to be analysed and the complexity of analysis, the Web Portal integrates suitable software for the management of different user groups, the content, the processing and presentation of data collected. The ESCOCITY Web Portal is addressed to the following users groups: "Mayor and advisors", "Municipal technical services", "Municipal accounting services", "Municipal employees" and "Citizens/Public users". Each user group has jurisdiction at specific areas of the energy management platform along with the relevant rights (Marinakis et al., 2015a).

The data is collected from the appropriate metering equipment and are handled by the following platform tools (Marinakis et al., 2015b):

- Green Buildings Tool collects, analyses and presents data concerning the buildings' energy management (building's energy consumption, environmental impact, economic impact etc.);
- Green Pillars/Pole Tool focuses on the street and road lighting control, by the following: voltage control supplied to the lighting circuit; operating lights efficiently by user defined time schedules; collecting data on street lighting, analysing the lamps' failures and reports crucial data for the user;
- Green EV Station Support Tool processes data for EV charging stations, namely those parking spaces where EV supply equipment will be used to charge vehicles.

Comparative Analysis

An overview of the main advantages of each tool is provided in Table 2. More specifically, both tools have a web-based environment and data integration process, in order to collect data from different sources. The DSS collects data from five multidisciplinary sources though the relevant data capturing modules developed. The Web Portal collects data from metering devices, which measure the energy data in the municipal buildings and the relevant infrastructures.

Furthermore, another difference is that the DSS processes the data through prediction models and inference rules, in order to propose specific short term Action Plans to the end users. On the other hand, the Web Portal uses the collected data to perform energy management, providing alerts to the end users for the proper operation of the city's infrastructure.

Finally, the Web Portal addresses all the municipal buildings and infrastructures, street lighting, electric vehicle. The web-based DSS gives particular emphasis on the municipal buildings and the renewable energy production and storage linked to the buildings.

Table 2. Comparative analysis of web-based DSS and web portal

	Web-Based DSS	Web Portal
Data integration process	x (developed using Semantic Web technologies)	X (Central gateway and OPC server, by MODBUS protocol)
Weather forecasting	x (data capturing module)	-
Social data	x (data capturing module)	-
Energy prices	x (data capturing module)	-
De-centralized sensor-based	x (data capturing module)	x (from metering devices)
Renewable energy production	x (data capturing module)	x (from metering devices)
Data processing	x (prediction models and inference rules)	-
Energy management	-	x (including alerts)
Proposed actions	x	-
Web environment	x	x
Buildings	x	x
Lighting	-	x
Vehicles	-	x
RES production, storage, etc.	x (linked to the buildings)	x

CONCLUSION

Since cities can influence over 70% of the total ecological footprint they have to take innovative actions in order to assist the implementation of Europe 2020 initiatives. One of these actions is to foster energy efficient neighbourhoods with the use of innovative ICTs. Currently there are plenty of energy related data available in the cities, but there are no established methodologies and validated tools to collect, integrate and analyse them.

This Chapter presented the "Smart Cities IoT Platform". In this context, two innovative ICT solutions were presented, namely the web-based DSS and the integrated Web Portal:

- DSS achieves the collection of data from five heterogeneous data sources (weather conditions, social mining, buildings' energy profiles, energy prices, energy production), integrates the using Semantic technologies, and proposed short term Action Plans to the local authorities;
- The Web Portal collects and integrates data from buildings and infrastructures of a given municipality, based on the available tools "Green Buildings", "Green Pillars", "Green Pole" and "Green Electric Vehicle Station Support". The Portal's users are classified into five different groups each one with relevant rights and responsibilities.

The proposed IoT Platform has, by design, the necessary degree of generalization, so as to be easily adapted to different sectors and cities, with different characteristics, energy infrastructures, needs, priorities and types of energy demand.

ACKNOWLEDGMENT

This chapter is based on the research conducted within the following two projects: (a) "OPTIMising the energy USe in cities with smart decision support system (OPTIMUS)" (grant agreement n° 608703), which has received funding from the European Union Seventh Framework Programme (FP7/2007-2013); (b) "ESCO Smart City Energy Plan (ESCOCITY)" (project number: ΓΓΕΤ ISR_3108), supported by the General Secretariat for Research and Technology (GSRT) of the Hellenic Ministry of Culture, Education and Religious Affairs. The content of the paper is a sole responsibility of its authors and does not necessarily reflect the views of the EC.

REFERENCES

Androulaki, S., Doukas, H., Marinakis, V., Madrazo, L., & Legaki, N. Z. (2016). Enabling Local Authorities to Produce Short-Term Energy Plans: A Multidisciplinary Decision Support Approach. *Management of Environmental Quality, 27*(2), 146–166. doi:10.1108/MEQ-02-2014-0021

Attia, S., & Carlucci, S. (2015). Impact of different thermal comfort models on zero energy residential buildings in hot climate. *Energy and Building, 102*, 117–128. doi:10.1016/j.enbuild.2015.05.017

Brandemuehl, M., & Braun, J. (1999). *The Impact of Demand-Controlled and Economizer Ventilation Strategies on Energy Use in Buildings*. Retrieved February 21, 2016, from: https://customer.honeywell.com/resources/techlit/TechLitDocuments/63-0000s/63-7063.pdf

Brooklyn Microgrid. (2017). Retrieved from http://www.brooklynmicrogrid.com

Cano, E. L., Javier, M. M., Ermolieva, T., & Ermoliev, Y. (2013). *Energy Efficiency and Risk Management in Public Buildings: Strategic Model for Robust Planning*. Computational Management Science.

Capozzoli, A., Corrado, V., Doukas, H., Gorrino, A., Piscitelli, M., Rossi, M., & Spiliotis, V. (2016). *Impact Analysis Report*. Deliverable 4.7 of the OPTIMUS Project.

Dassani, N., Nirwan, D., & Hariharan, G. (2015). *Dubai – a new paradigm for smart cities*. KPMG Report. Retrieved January 18, 2017, from: https://assets.kpmg.com/content/dam/kpmg/pdf/2016/04/Dubai-a-new-paradigm-for-smart-cities-uae.pdf

Doukas, H., Marinakis, V., Spiliotis, V., & Psarras, J. (2017). *OPTIMUS Decision Support Tools: Transforming Multidisciplinary Data to Energy Management Action Plans*. IEEE - 7th International Conference on Information, Intelligence, Systems and Applications (IISA 2016).

Doyle, S. (2009). *Data Mapping, Modeling and Experimental Simulation as Information Management Tools in Urban System and Infrastructure Design*. Zofnass Program for Infrastructure Sustainabilit.

ESMAP (Energy Sector Management Assistance Program), World Bank. (2010). *Rapid Assessment Framework, An Innovative Decision Support Tool for Evaluating Energy Efficiency Opportunities in Cities.* Report No. 57685. Author.

Falleni, C. (2016). *A machine-driven future and the imminent need for basic income: Self-Driving vehicles will not only create new mobility patterns but will reshape cities and economic systems.* Retrieved February 11, 2017, from: https://medium.com/@caterinafalleni/a-machine-driven-future-and-the-imminent-need-for-basic-income-3b9ea412d3ca#.qp2t0uq2x

Fernandez, N., Katipamula, S., Wang, W., Huang, Y., & Liu, G. (2012). *Energy Savings Modeling of Standard Commercial Building Re-tuning Measures: Large Office Buildings.* U.S. Department of Energy. Retrieved December 13, 2016, from: http://www.pnnl.gov/buildingretuning/documents/pnnl_21569.pdf

Fluhr, J.W., & Williams, F. (2011). *FINSENY: Future Internet for Smart Energy.* Unternehmen der Zukunft 2/2011.

Frost & Sullivan. (2017). *Urbanization Trends in 2020: Mega Cities and Smart Cities Built on a Vision of Sustainability.* Retrieved December 13, 2016, from: http://www.frost.com/prod/servlet/cpo/213304107.pdf

GeSI – Global e-Sustainability Initiative. (2015). *#SMARTer2030 – ICT Solutions for 21st Century Challenges.* Retrieved January 18, 2017, from: http://smarter2030.gesi.org/downloads/Full_report.pdf

Grabar, H. (2016). *How Will Self-Driving Cars Change Cities? Slate.* Retrieved December 13, 2016, from: http://www.slate.com/articles/health_and_science/medical_examiner/2017/02/going_undercover_through_washington_s_revolving_door.html

Green, S. (2017). Even buildings are going the way of big data: Future abundance of smart properties will lead to more data and associated risks. *Gulf News Property.* Retrieved February 11, 2017, from: http://gulfnews.com/business/property/even-buildings-are-going-the-way-of-big-data-1.1975040?platform=hootsuite

Guan, X., Xu, Z., & Jia, Q.-S. (2010). Energy-Efficient Buildings Facilitated by Microgrid. *IEEE Transactions on Smart Grid, 1*(3), 243–252. doi:10.1109/TSG.2010.2083705

Kwang, T. W. (2016). *A look into Dubai's smart city initiatives. eGov Innovation*. Retrieved February 11, 2017, from: http://www.enterpriseinnovation.net/article/look-dubais-smart-city-initiatives-1141254266

Lima, J. (2016). 5 of the biggest Internet of Things smart city projects from around the world. *CBR – Computer Business Review*. Retrieved February 11, 2017, from: http://www.cbronline.com/news/internet-of-things/5-mega-smart-city-projects-from-around-the-world-4881856/

Maloney, P. (2016). *Siemens, LO3 Energy teams up for blockchain-powered microgrid in Brooklyn*. Retrieved February 11, 2017, from: http://www.utilitydive.com/news/siemens-lo3-energy-teams-up-for-blockchain-powered-microgrid-in-brooklyn/430884/

Marinakis, V., Papadopoulou, A., Anastasopoulos, G., Doukas, H., & Psarras, J. (2015b). *Advanced ICT Platform for Real-time Monitoring and Infrastructure Efficiency at the City Level*. The 6th International Conference on Information, Intelligence, Systems and Applications (IISA 2015), Corfu, Greece. doi:10.1109/IISA.2015.7387958

Marinakis, V., Papadopoulou, A. G., Anastasopoulos, G., Doukas, H., & Psarras, J. (2015a). *Energy Management Services for the City Authorities: The ESCOCITY Web Portal*. 4th International Symposium and 26th National Conference on Operational Research, Chania, Greece.

Mastrodonato, C., Cavallaro, A., Hannus, M., Nummelin, J., & Jung, N. (2011). ICT for Energy Efficient Buildings: Proposed approach for a stakeholders-based strategic roadmap. *Proceedings of the CIB W78 W102 2011: International Conference.*

ME CONSTRUCION NEWS. (2017). *Smart grids 'can save GCC countries $10bn by 2020'*. Retrieved February 11, 2017, from: http://meconstructionnews.com/20745/smart-grids-can-save-gcc-countries-10bn-by-2020?platform=hootsuite

Mihaylov, M. (2015). *Digital currency for green energy can boost the renewable economy*. Retrieved February 11, 2017, from: http://www.focas-reading-room.eu/digital-currency-for-green-energy-can-boost-the-renewable-economy

Moeseke, G., Bruyère, I., & De Herde, A. (2007). Impact of control rules on the efficiency of shading devices and free cooling for office buildings. *Building and Environment, 42*(2), 784–793. doi:10.1016/j.buildenv.2005.09.015

OPTIMUS. (2014). Retrieved from http://optimus-smartcity.eu/optimus-dss

Page, J., Basciotti, D., Pol, O., Fidalgo, J. N., Couto, M., Aron, R., . . . Fournie, L. (2013). A multi-energy modeling, simulation and optimization environment for urban energy infrastructure planning. *Proceedings of BS2013, 13th Conference of International Building Performance Simulation Association.*

Papastamatiou, I., Doukas, H., Spiliotis, E., & Psarras, J. (2016). How OPTIMUS is a city in terms of energy optimization? e-SCEAF: A web based decision support tool for local authorities. *Information Fusion, 29,* 149–161. doi:10.1016/j.inffus.2015.10.002

Patti, D., de Amicis, R., Prandi, F., D'Hondt, E., Rudolf, H., Elisei, P., & Saghin, I. (2013). iScope Smart Cities and Citizens. *REAL-CORP 2013 Proceedings.*

Periodic Report Summary. (2013). Retrieved February 11, 2017, from: http://cordis.europa.eu/result/report/rcn/54817_en.html

Power, D. (2016). *Will autonomous microgrids drive IoT in smart cities?.* Retrieved February 11, 2017, from: http://readwrite.com/2016/10/05/microgrids-will-boost-iot-adoption-smart-cities-cl1/

Rutkin, A. (2016). *Blockchain-based microgrid gives power to consumers in New York.* Retrieved February 11, 2017, from: https://www.newscientist.com/article/2079334-blockchain-based-microgrid-gives-power-to-consumers-in-new-york/

Sala, M., Gallo, C., & Sayigh, A. A. M. (1999). Architecture - Comfort & Energy. Elsevier.

SEMANCO Project Methodology Report. (2012). *FP7/287534, "Semantic Tools for Carbon Reduction in Urban Planning".* Author.

Smith, A., & Gordon, G. (2017). *Masdar City, a zero-waste, zero-carbon city in the desert.* Retrieved February 11, 2017, from: http://living-circular.com/en/lifestyle/masdar-city-zero-waste-and-zero-carbon-desert

Steen, D., Tuan, A., & Bertling, L. (2016). *Price-Based Demand-Side Management for Reducing Peak Demand in Electrical Distribution Systems – With Examples from Gothenburg.* Retrieved February 11, 2017, from: http://publications.lib.chalmers.se/records/fulltext/163330/local_163330.pdf

UNC. (2016). *A Method for Calculating Chilled Water and Steam Energy Savings Due to Occupancy Scheduling in Large Buildings with Only One Year of Data.* Retrieved February 11, 2017, from: https://save-energy. unc.edu/Portals/2/Calculating%20Occupancy%20Schedule%20Savings. pdf?ver=2012-10-26-133759-960

Watts, J. M., & Purnell, N. (2016). Singapore Is Taking the 'Smart City' to a Whole New Level. *The Wall Street Journal.* Retrieved February 11, 2017, from: https://www.wsj.com/articles/singapore-is-taking-the-smart-city-to-a-whole-new-level-1461550026

Woods, E. (2016). *How Smart Cities are Accelerating the Energy Transition.* Navigant Research. Retrieved January 18, 2017, from: https://www.navigant. com/insights/energy/2016/smart-cities-energy-transition

Yang, Z., & Becerik-Gerber, B. (2014). The coupled effects of personalized occupancy profile based HVAC schedules and room reassignment on building energy use. *Energy and Building*, *78*, 113–122. doi:10.1016/j. enbuild.2014.04.002

ENDNOTE

[1] Natural gas feeding the microturbines of the SPM for the production of both thermal energy and electricity (754 MWh) and thermal energy produced by two natural gas boilers (607 MWh).

Related Readings

To continue IGI Global's long-standing tradition of advancing innovation through emerging research, please find below a compiled list of recommended IGI Global book chapters and journal articles in the areas of energy planning, climate change, and efficient energy. These related readings will provide additional information and guidance to further enrich your knowledge and assist you with your own research.

Adler, M. (2015). Floods Monitoring. In C. Maftei (Ed.), *Extreme Weather and Impacts of Climate Change on Water Resources in the Dobrogea Region* (pp. 312–344). Hershey, PA: IGI Global. doi:10.4018/978-1-4666-8438-6.ch011

Afzal, S. (2016). Implementation of Flooding Free Routing in Smart Grid: VCP Routing in Smart Gird. In A. Ahmad & N. Hassan (Eds.), *Smart Grid as a Solution for Renewable and Efficient Energy* (pp. 298–322). Hershey, PA: IGI Global. doi:10.4018/978-1-5225-0072-8.ch013

Ahmad, S., Ahmad, A., & Yaqub, R. (2016). Optimized Energy Consumption and Demand Side Management in Smart Grid. In A. Ahmad & N. Hassan (Eds.), *Smart Grid as a Solution for Renewable and Efficient Energy* (pp. 1–25). Hershey, PA: IGI Global. doi:10.4018/978-1-5225-0072-8.ch001

Arbaiy, N., Watada, J., & Lin, P. (2016). Fuzzy Random Regression-Based Modeling in Uncertain Environment. In P. Vasant & N. Voropai (Eds.), *Sustaining Power Resources through Energy Optimization and Engineering* (pp. 127–146). Hershey, PA: IGI Global. doi:10.4018/978-1-4666-9755-3.ch006

Arhin, A. (2016). Improving Sustainability of the Environment in a Changing Climate: Can REDD+ Rise to the Challenge? In S. Dinda (Ed.), *Handbook of Research on Climate Change Impact on Health and Environmental Sustainability* (pp. 327–346). Hershey, PA: IGI Global. doi:10.4018/978-1-4666-8814-8.ch016

Bahinipati, C. S., Patnaik, U., & Viswanathan, P. K. (2016). What Causes Economic Losses from Natural Disasters in India? In S. Dinda (Ed.), *Handbook of Research on Climate Change Impact on Health and Environmental Sustainability* (pp. 157–175). Hershey, PA: IGI Global. doi:10.4018/978-1-4666-8814-8.ch008

Banerjee, S. (2016). Social Innovation: A Theoretical Approach in Intertwining Climate Change with Social Innovation. In S. Dinda (Ed.), *Handbook of Research on Climate Change Impact on Health and Environmental Sustainability* (pp. 593–618). Hershey, PA: IGI Global. doi:10.4018/978-1-4666-8814-8.ch029

Barakabitze, A. A., Fue, K. G., Kitindi, E. J., & Sanga, C. A. (2016). Developing a Framework for Next Generation Integrated Agro Food-Advisory Systems in Developing Countries. *International Journal of Information Communication Technologies and Human Development*, 8(4), 13–31. doi:10.4018/IJICTHD.2016100102

Basu, J. P. (2016). Coastal Poverty, Resource-Dependent Livelihood, Climate Change, and Adaptation: An Empirical Study in Indian Coastal Sunderbans. In S. Dinda (Ed.), *Handbook of Research on Climate Change Impact on Health and Environmental Sustainability* (pp. 441–454). Hershey, PA: IGI Global. doi:10.4018/978-1-4666-8814-8.ch022

Bekele, I., & Ganpat, W. (2015). Education, Extension, and Training for Climate Change. In W. Ganpat & W. Isaac (Eds.), *Impacts of Climate Change on Food Security in Small Island Developing States* (pp. 361–388). Hershey, PA: IGI Global. doi:10.4018/978-1-4666-6501-9.ch012

Bhaskar, A., Rao, G. B., & Vencatesan, J. (2017). Characterization and Management Concerns of Water Resources around Pallikaranai Marsh, South Chennai. In P. Rao & Y. Patil (Eds.), *Reconsidering the Impact of Climate Change on Global Water Supply, Use, and Management* (pp. 102–121). Hershey, PA: IGI Global. doi:10.4018/978-1-5225-1046-8.ch007

Bhatt, R. (2017). Zero Tillage for Mitigating Global Warming Consequences and Improving Livelihoods in South Asia. In W. Ganpat & W. Isaac (Eds.), *Environmental Sustainability and Climate Change Adaptation Strategies* (pp. 126–161). Hershey, PA: IGI Global. doi:10.4018/978-1-5225-1607-1.ch005

Bit, J., & Banerjee, S. (2016). Sustainable Forest Use and India's Economic Growth: A Structural Decomposition Analysis of Direct Forest Intensity. In S. Dinda (Ed.), *Handbook of Research on Climate Change Impact on Health and Environmental Sustainability* (pp. 306–326). Hershey, PA: IGI Global. doi:10.4018/978-1-4666-8814-8.ch015

Boonkerd, K. (2017). Development and Modification of Natural Rubber for Advanced Application. In T. Kobayashi (Ed.), *Applied Environmental Materials Science for Sustainability* (pp. 44–76). Hershey, PA: IGI Global. doi:10.4018/978-1-5225-1971-3.ch003

Boonmahitthisud, A. (2017). Natural Rubber and Rubber Blend Nanocomposites: Reinforcement of Natural Rubber with Polymer-Encapsulated Inorganic Nanohybrid Particles. In T. Kobayashi (Ed.), *Applied Environmental Materials Science for Sustainability* (pp. 77–105). Hershey, PA: IGI Global. doi:10.4018/978-1-5225-1971-3.ch004

Bostanci, S. H., & Albayrak, A. N. (2017). The Role of Eco-Municipalities in Climate Change for a Sustainable Future. In W. Ganpat & W. Isaac (Eds.), *Environmental Sustainability and Climate Change Adaptation Strategies* (pp. 213–231). Hershey, PA: IGI Global. doi:10.4018/978-1-5225-1607-1.ch008

Buta, C., Omer, I., & Andronic, A. (2015). Hydrological Risk Phenomena and Flood Analysis: Study Case – Taita Catchment, Romania. In C. Maftei (Ed.), *Extreme Weather and Impacts of Climate Change on Water Resources in the Dobrogea Region* (pp. 284–311). Hershey, PA: IGI Global. doi:10.4018/978-1-4666-8438-6.ch010

Carrillo, K. L., & Kobayashi, T. (2017). Natural Material Source of Bagasse Cellulose and Their Application to Hydrogel Films. In T. Kobayashi (Ed.), *Applied Environmental Materials Science for Sustainability* (pp. 19–43). Hershey, PA: IGI Global. doi:10.4018/978-1-5225-1971-3.ch002

Cazacu, G. B. (2015). Dobrogea Geology. In C. Maftei (Ed.), *Extreme Weather and Impacts of Climate Change on Water Resources in the Dobrogea Region* (pp. 73–118). Hershey, PA: IGI Global. doi:10.4018/978-1-4666-8438-6.ch004

Chai-Ittipornwong, T. (2017). Participation Framework to Sustainability: The Undercurrents in Bottled-Water Production and Consumption. In P. Rao & Y. Patil (Eds.), *Reconsidering the Impact of Climate Change on Global Water Supply, Use, and Management* (pp. 272–293). Hershey, PA: IGI Global. doi:10.4018/978-1-5225-1046-8.ch015

Chatterjee, T., & Dinda, S. (2016). Climate Change, Human Health and Some Economic Issues. In S. Dinda (Ed.), *Handbook of Research on Climate Change Impact on Health and Environmental Sustainability* (pp. 26–41). Hershey, PA: IGI Global. doi:10.4018/978-1-4666-8814-8.ch002

Chaudhary, N., & Pisolkar, Y. (2017). Issues, Concerns, and Local Stakes: Future of Water Resources in Coastal Villages of Devbag and Tarkarli, Coastal Maharashtra, India. In P. Rao & Y. Patil (Eds.), *Reconsidering the Impact of Climate Change on Global Water Supply, Use, and Management* (pp. 50–69). Hershey, PA: IGI Global. doi:10.4018/978-1-5225-1046-8.ch004

Chelcea, S., Ionita, M., & Adler, M. (2015). Identification of Dry Periods in the Dobrogea Region. In C. Maftei (Ed.), *Extreme Weather and Impacts of Climate Change on Water Resources in the Dobrogea Region* (pp. 52–72). Hershey, PA: IGI Global. doi:10.4018/978-1-4666-8438-6.ch003

Cohen, J. E., Clarke-Harris, D. O., Khan, A., & Isaac, W. P. (2015). Sustainable Management of Invasive Species for Small Island Developing States under Changing Climates. In W. Ganpat & W. Isaac (Eds.), *Impacts of Climate Change on Food Security in Small Island Developing States* (pp. 312–360). Hershey, PA: IGI Global. doi:10.4018/978-1-4666-6501-9.ch011

Das, S. (2016). Health Impact of Water-Related Diseases in Developing Countries on Account of Climate Change – A Systematic Review: A Study in Regard to South Asian Countries. In S. Dinda (Ed.), *Handbook of Research on Climate Change Impact on Health and Environmental Sustainability* (pp. 42–60). Hershey, PA: IGI Global. doi:10.4018/978-1-4666-8814-8.ch003

David, I., Beilicci, E., & Beilicci, R. (2015). Basics for Hydraulic Modelling of Flood Runoff Using Advanced Hydroinformatic Tools. In C. Maftei (Ed.), *Extreme Weather and Impacts of Climate Change on Water Resources in the Dobrogea Region* (pp. 205–239). Hershey, PA: IGI Global. doi:10.4018/978-1-4666-8438-6.ch008

Deenapanray, P. N., & Ramma, I. (2015). Adaptations to Climate Change and Climate Variability in the Agriculture Sector in Mauritius: Lessons from a Technical Needs Assessment. In W. Ganpat & W. Isaac (Eds.), *Impacts of Climate Change on Food Security in Small Island Developing States* (pp. 130–165). Hershey, PA: IGI Global. doi:10.4018/978-1-4666-6501-9.ch005

Dinda, S. (2016). Adaptation to Climate Change for Sustainable Development: A Survey. In S. Dinda (Ed.), *Handbook of Research on Climate Change Impact on Health and Environmental Sustainability* (pp. 363–391). Hershey, PA: IGI Global. doi:10.4018/978-1-4666-8814-8.ch018

Dinda, S. (2016). Climate Change, Trade Competitiveness, and Opportunity for Climate Friendly Goods in SAARC and Asia Pacific Regions. In S. Dinda (Ed.), *Handbook of Research on Climate Change Impact on Health and Environmental Sustainability* (pp. 515–536). Hershey, PA: IGI Global. doi:10.4018/978-1-4666-8814-8.ch026

Dongol, D., Bollin, E., & Feldmann, T. (2016). Battery Management Based on Predictive Control and Demand-Side Management: Smart Integration of Renewable Energy Sources. In A. Ahmad & N. Hassan (Eds.), *Smart Grid as a Solution for Renewable and Efficient Energy* (pp. 149–180). Hershey, PA: IGI Global. doi:10.4018/978-1-5225-0072-8.ch007

Drăguşin, D. (2015). Drought Effects on Groundwater in Dobrogea Plateau. In C. Maftei (Ed.), *Extreme Weather and Impacts of Climate Change on Water Resources in the Dobrogea Region* (pp. 119–144). Hershey, PA: IGI Global. doi:10.4018/978-1-4666-8438-6.ch005

Elsayed, A. M., Dakkama, H. J., Mahmoud, S., Al-Dadah, R., & Kaialy, W. (2017). Sustainable Cooling Research Using Activated Carbon Adsorbents and Their Environmental Impact. In T. Kobayashi (Ed.), *Applied Environmental Materials Science for Sustainability* (pp. 186–221). Hershey, PA: IGI Global. doi:10.4018/978-1-5225-1971-3.ch009

Emmanuel, M., Muasa, L., Chen, C., Mutisya, F., & Avtar, R. (2016). Impact of Rapid Urbanization and Climate Change on Agricultural Productivity in Africa: Climate Change Policies in the Agricultural Sector. In S. Dinda (Ed.), *Handbook of Research on Climate Change Impact on Health and Environmental Sustainability* (pp. 416–426). Hershey, PA: IGI Global. doi:10.4018/978-1-4666-8814-8.ch020

Related Readings

Emran, A., Rob, M. A., & Kabir, M. H. (2017). Coastline Change and Erosion-Accretion Evolution of the Sandwip Island, Bangladesh. *International Journal of Applied Geospatial Research, 8*(2), 33–44. doi:10.4018/IJAGR.2017040103

Eudoxie, G., & Roopnarine, R. (2017). Climate Change Adaptation and Disaster Risk Management in the Caribbean. In W. Ganpat & W. Isaac (Eds.), *Environmental Sustainability and Climate Change Adaptation Strategies* (pp. 97–125). Hershey, PA: IGI Global. doi:10.4018/978-1-5225-1607-1.ch004

Eudoxie, G. D., & Wuddivira, M. (2015). Soil, Water, and Agricultural Adaptations. In W. Ganpat & W. Isaac (Eds.), *Impacts of Climate Change on Food Security in Small Island Developing States* (pp. 255–279). Hershey, PA: IGI Global. doi:10.4018/978-1-4666-6501-9.ch009

Fernández, F. J., Jiménez, A. D., Manzano, F. S., & Márquez, J. M. (2017). An Energy Management Strategy and Fuel Cell Configuration Proposal for a Hybrid Renewable System with Hydrogen Backup. *International Journal of Energy Optimization and Engineering, 6*(1), 1–22. doi:10.4018/IJEOE.2017010101

Fernando, Y., & Wah, W. X. (2016). Moving forward a Parsimonious Model of Eco-Innovation: Results from a Content Analysis. In S. Dinda (Ed.), *Handbook of Research on Climate Change Impact on Health and Environmental Sustainability* (pp. 619–631). Hershey, PA: IGI Global. doi:10.4018/978-1-4666-8814-8.ch030

Garrick, T. A., & Liburd, O. E. (2017). Impact of Climate Change on a Key Agricultural Pest: Thrips. In W. Ganpat & W. Isaac (Eds.), *Environmental Sustainability and Climate Change Adaptation Strategies* (pp. 232–254). Hershey, PA: IGI Global. doi:10.4018/978-1-5225-1607-1.ch009

Goundar, S., & Appana, S. (2017). Mainstreaming Development Policies for Climate Change in Fiji: A Policy Gap Analysis and the Role of ICTs. In W. Ganpat & W. Isaac (Eds.), *Environmental Sustainability and Climate Change Adaptation Strategies* (pp. 1–31). Hershey, PA: IGI Global. doi:10.4018/978-1-5225-1607-1.ch001

Gupta, A. C. (2016). Bioeconomic Fishery Management: Changing Paradigms towards Eco-System Based Management. In S. Dinda (Ed.), *Handbook of Research on Climate Change Impact on Health and Environmental Sustainability* (pp. 261–281). Hershey, PA: IGI Global. doi:10.4018/978-1-4666-8814-8.ch013

Hiremath, R., Kumar, B., Bansode, S. S., Nulkar, G., Patil, S. S., & Murali, J. (2017). Industrial Wastewater Management in the Context of Climate Change Adaptation in Selected Cities of India: A Business Approach. In P. Rao & Y. Patil (Eds.), *Reconsidering the Impact of Climate Change on Global Water Supply, Use, and Management* (pp. 294–313). Hershey, PA: IGI Global. doi:10.4018/978-1-5225-1046-8.ch016

Huyen, P. T. (2017). Clay Minerals Converted to Porous Materials and Their Application: Challenge and Perspective. In T. Kobayashi (Ed.), *Applied Environmental Materials Science for Sustainability* (pp. 141–164). Hershey, PA: IGI Global. doi:10.4018/978-1-5225-1971-3.ch007

Iese, V., Maeke, J., Holland, E., Wairiu, M., & Naidu, S. (2015). Farming Adaptations to the Impacts of Climate Change and Extreme Events in Pacific Island Countries: Case Study of Bellona Atoll, Solomon Islands. In W. Ganpat & W. Isaac (Eds.), *Impacts of Climate Change on Food Security in Small Island Developing States* (pp. 166–194). Hershey, PA: IGI Global. doi:10.4018/978-1-4666-6501-9.ch006

Ikematsu, S., Tada, I., & Nagasaki, Y. (2017). Analysis of Lipids Produced by Microalgae Isolated from the Area around Okinawa, Japan. In T. Kobayashi (Ed.), *Applied Environmental Materials Science for Sustainability* (pp. 222–233). Hershey, PA: IGI Global. doi:10.4018/978-1-5225-1971-3.ch010

Inogwabini, B. (2017). Congo Basin's Shrinking Watersheds: Potential Consequences on Local Communities. In P. Rao & Y. Patil (Eds.), *Reconsidering the Impact of Climate Change on Global Water Supply, Use, and Management* (pp. 211–226). Hershey, PA: IGI Global. doi:10.4018/978-1-5225-1046-8.ch012

Ionita, M., & Chelcea, S. (2015). Spatio-Temporal Variability of Seasonal Drought over the Dobrogea Region. In C. Maftei (Ed.), *Extreme Weather and Impacts of Climate Change on Water Resources in the Dobrogea Region* (pp. 17–51). Hershey, PA: IGI Global. doi:10.4018/978-1-4666-8438-6.ch002

Issakhov, A. (2016). Mathematical Modelling of the Thermal Process in the Aquatic Environment with Considering the Hydrometeorological Condition at the Reservoir-Cooler by Using Parallel Technologies. In P. Vasant & N. Voropai (Eds.), *Sustaining Power Resources through Energy Optimization and Engineering* (pp. 227–243). Hershey, PA: IGI Global. doi:10.4018/978-1-4666-9755-3.ch010

Javid, T. (2016). Geographic Information System for the Smart Grid. In A. Ahmad & N. Hassan (Eds.), *Smart Grid as a Solution for Renewable and Efficient Energy* (pp. 344–362). Hershey, PA: IGI Global. doi:10.4018/978-1-5225-0072-8.ch015

Juma, D. W., Reuben, M., Wang, H., & Li, F. (2017). Adaptive Coevolution: Realigning the Water Governance Regime to the Changing Climate. In P. Rao & Y. Patil (Eds.), *Reconsidering the Impact of Climate Change on Global Water Supply, Use, and Management* (pp. 314–325). Hershey, PA: IGI Global. doi:10.4018/978-1-5225-1046-8.ch017

Kais, S. M. (2017). Climate Change: Vulnerability and Resilience in Commercial Shrimp Aquaculture in Bangladesh. In W. Ganpat & W. Isaac (Eds.), *Environmental Sustainability and Climate Change Adaptation Strategies* (pp. 162–187). Hershey, PA: IGI Global. doi:10.4018/978-1-5225-1607-1.ch006

Kamboj, V. K., & Bath, S. K. (2016). Scope of Biogeography-Based Optimization for Economic Load Dispatch and Multi-Objective Unit Commitment Problem. In P. Vasant & N. Voropai (Eds.), *Sustaining Power Resources through Energy Optimization and Engineering* (pp. 360–389). Hershey, PA: IGI Global. doi:10.4018/978-1-4666-9755-3.ch015

Karmaoui, A. (2016). Environmental Vulnerability to Climate Change in Mediterranean Basin: Socio-Ecological Interactions between North and South. In S. Dinda (Ed.), *Handbook of Research on Climate Change Impact on Health and Environmental Sustainability* (pp. 105–138). Hershey, PA: IGI Global. doi:10.4018/978-1-4666-8814-8.ch006

Khai, H. V. (2016). Assessing Urban Residents' Willingness to Pay for Preserving the Biodiversity of Swamp Forest. In S. Dinda (Ed.), *Handbook of Research on Climate Change Impact on Health and Environmental Sustainability* (pp. 283–305). Hershey, PA: IGI Global. doi:10.4018/978-1-4666-8814-8.ch014

Khalid, S. (2016). Application of Adaptive Tabu Search Algorithm in Hybrid Power Filter and Shunt Active Power Filters: Application of ATS Algorithm in HPF and APF. In P. Vasant & N. Voropai (Eds.), *Sustaining Power Resources through Energy Optimization and Engineering* (pp. 276–308). Hershey, PA: IGI Global. doi:10.4018/978-1-4666-9755-3.ch012

Khan, S. S. (2016). Modeling and Operating Strategies of Micro-Grids for Renewable Energy Communities. In A. Ahmad & N. Hassan (Eds.), *Smart Grid as a Solution for Renewable and Efficient Energy* (pp. 97–122). Hershey, PA: IGI Global. doi:10.4018/978-1-5225-0072-8.ch005

Khanna, B. K. (2017). Indian National Strategy for Climate Change Adaptation and Mitigation. In W. Ganpat & W. Isaac (Eds.), *Environmental Sustainability and Climate Change Adaptation Strategies* (pp. 32–63). Hershey, PA: IGI Global. doi:10.4018/978-1-5225-1607-1.ch002

Khanna, B. K. (2017). Vulnerability of the Lakshadweep Coral Islands in India and Strategies for Mitigating Climate Change Impacts. In W. Ganpat & W. Isaac (Eds.), *Environmental Sustainability and Climate Change Adaptation Strategies* (pp. 64–96). Hershey, PA: IGI Global. doi:10.4018/978-1-5225-1607-1.ch003

Kobayashi, T. (2017). Introduction of Environmental Materials. In T. Kobayashi (Ed.), *Applied Environmental Materials Science for Sustainability* (pp. 1–18). Hershey, PA: IGI Global. doi:10.4018/978-1-5225-1971-3.ch001

Kumar, C. P. (2016). Impact of Climate Change on Groundwater Resources. In S. Dinda (Ed.), *Handbook of Research on Climate Change Impact on Health and Environmental Sustainability* (pp. 196–221). Hershey, PA: IGI Global. doi:10.4018/978-1-4666-8814-8.ch010

Kumar, K. V., Kumar, S. S., Selvakumar, A. I., & Kumar, R. S. (2016). Recent Techniques to Identify the Stator Fault Diagnosis in Three Phase Induction Motor. In P. Vasant & N. Voropai (Eds.), *Sustaining Power Resources through Energy Optimization and Engineering* (pp. 309–325). Hershey, PA: IGI Global. doi:10.4018/978-1-4666-9755-3.ch013

Kumar, M. (2016). Environmental Sustainability in the Fashion Supply Chain in India. *International Journal of Social Ecology and Sustainable Development*, 7(3), 1–33. doi:10.4018/IJSESD.2016070101

Kumar, M. (2017). Economic Evaluation of Solar Cooling Schemes. *International Journal of Energy Optimization and Engineering*, 6(1), 23–48. doi:10.4018/IJEOE.2017010102

Kumar, R., Rao, P., & Areendran, G. (2017). Understanding Glacial Retreat in the Indian Himalaya: Historical Trends and Field Studies from a Large Glacier. In P. Rao & Y. Patil (Eds.), *Reconsidering the Impact of Climate Change on Global Water Supply, Use, and Management* (pp. 33–49). Hershey, PA: IGI Global. doi:10.4018/978-1-5225-1046-8.ch003

Kumari, S., & Patil, Y. (2017). Achieving Climate Smart Agriculture with a Sustainable Use of Water: A Conceptual Framework for Sustaining the Use of Water for Agriculture in the Era of Climate Change. In P. Rao & Y. Patil (Eds.), *Reconsidering the Impact of Climate Change on Global Water Supply, Use, and Management* (pp. 122–143). Hershey, PA: IGI Global. doi:10.4018/978-1-5225-1046-8.ch008

Kumari, S., Patil, Y., & Rao, P. (2017). An Approach to Sustainable Watershed Management: Case Studies on Enhancing Sustainability with Challenges of Water in Western Maharashtra. In P. Rao & Y. Patil (Eds.), *Reconsidering the Impact of Climate Change on Global Water Supply, Use, and Management* (pp. 252–271). Hershey, PA: IGI Global. doi:10.4018/978-1-5225-1046-8.ch014

Lallo, C. H., Smalling, S., Facey, A., & Hughes, M. (2017). The Impact of Climate Change on Small Ruminant Performance in Caribbean Communities. In W. Ganpat & W. Isaac (Eds.), *Environmental Sustainability and Climate Change Adaptation Strategies* (pp. 296–321). Hershey, PA: IGI Global. doi:10.4018/978-1-5225-1607-1.ch011

Lawrence, J., Simpson, L., & Piggott, A. (2015). Protected Agriculture: A Climate Change Adaptation for Food and Nutrition Security. In W. Ganpat & W. Isaac (Eds.), *Impacts of Climate Change on Food Security in Small Island Developing States* (pp. 196–220). Hershey, PA: IGI Global. doi:10.4018/978-1-4666-6501-9.ch007

Li, K., & Kobayashi, T. (2017). Ionic Liquids and Poly (Ionic Liquid)s Used as Green Solvent and Ultrasound Responded Materials. In T. Kobayashi (Ed.), *Applied Environmental Materials Science for Sustainability* (pp. 327–346). Hershey, PA: IGI Global. doi:10.4018/978-1-5225-1971-3.ch015

Liapakis, A., Costopoulou, C., Tsiligiridis, T., & Sideridis, A. (2017). Studying Corporate Social Responsibility Activities in the Agri-Food Sector: The Greek Case. *International Journal of Agricultural and Environmental Information Systems*, 8(1), 1–13. doi:10.4018/IJAEIS.2017010101

Loi, N. K., Huyen, N. T., Tu, L. H., Tram, V. N., Liem, N. D., Dat, N. L., & Minh, D. N. et al. (2017). Sustainable Land Use and Watershed Management in Response to Climate Change Impacts: Case Study in Srepok Watershed, Central Highland of Vietnam. In W. Ganpat & W. Isaac (Eds.), *Environmental Sustainability and Climate Change Adaptation Strategies* (pp. 255–295). Hershey, PA: IGI Global. doi:10.4018/978-1-5225-1607-1.ch010

Londhe, S. (2016). Impact of Climate Change on Agriculture and Food Security. *International Journal of Disease Control and Containment for Sustainability, 1*(1), 32–46. doi:10.4018/IJDCCS.2016010103

Londhe, S. (2017). Inter Linkages of Water, Climate, and Agriculture. In P. Rao & Y. Patil (Eds.), *Reconsidering the Impact of Climate Change on Global Water Supply, Use, and Management* (pp. 166–194). Hershey, PA: IGI Global. doi:10.4018/978-1-5225-1046-8.ch010

Londhe, S. L. (2016). Climate Change and Agriculture: Impacts, Adoption, and Mitigation. In S. Dinda (Ed.), *Handbook of Research on Climate Change Impact on Health and Environmental Sustainability* (pp. 393–415). Hershey, PA: IGI Global. doi:10.4018/978-1-4666-8814-8.ch019

Maftei, C., & Papatheodorou, K. (2015). Mathematical Models Used for Hydrological Floodplain Modeling. In C. Maftei (Ed.), *Extreme Weather and Impacts of Climate Change on Water Resources in the Dobrogea Region* (pp. 240–283). Hershey, PA: IGI Global. doi:10.4018/978-1-4666-8438-6.ch009

Maharaj, R., Singh-Ackbarali, D., & Sankat, C. K. (2015). Postharvest Management Strategies. In W. Ganpat & W. Isaac (Eds.), *Impacts of Climate Change on Food Security in Small Island Developing States* (pp. 221–254). Hershey, PA: IGI Global. doi:10.4018/978-1-4666-6501-9.ch008

Mahboob, Q. (2016). Identification of Reliability Critical Items in Large and Complex Rail Electrical Networks. In A. Ahmad & N. Hassan (Eds.), *Smart Grid as a Solution for Renewable and Efficient Energy* (pp. 226–248). Hershey, PA: IGI Global. doi:10.4018/978-1-5225-0072-8.ch010

Mahmood, W. A., & Azarian, M. H. (2017). Inorganic-Organic Composite Materials from Liquid Natural Rubber and Epoxidised Natural Rubber Derivatives: Prospects and Applications. In T. Kobayashi (Ed.), *Applied Environmental Materials Science for Sustainability* (pp. 128–140). Hershey, PA: IGI Global. doi:10.4018/978-1-5225-1971-3.ch006

Majumder, J., Shah, P., & Kumar, S. (2016). Heat Stress Vulnerability among Indian Workmen. In S. Dinda (Ed.), *Handbook of Research on Climate Change Impact on Health and Environmental Sustainability* (pp. 61–80). Hershey, PA: IGI Global. doi:10.4018/978-1-4666-8814-8.ch004

Maximay, S. (2015). The Caribbean's Response to Climate Change Impacts. In W. Ganpat & W. Isaac (Eds.), *Impacts of Climate Change on Food Security in Small Island Developing States* (pp. 33–66). Hershey, PA: IGI Global. doi:10.4018/978-1-4666-6501-9.ch002

Meldrum, H. M., Szymanski, D., Oches, E. A., & Davis, P. T. (2016). A Picture is Worth a Thousand Words: Commentary of Broadcast Meteorologists on the Visual Presentation of Climate Change. *International Journal of Social Ecology and Sustainable Development*, 7(4), 1–16. doi:10.4018/IJSESD.2016100101

Mili, B., Barua, A., & Katyaini, S. (2016). Climate Change and Adaptation through the Lens of Capability Approach: A Case Study from Darjeeling, Eastern Himalaya. In S. Dinda (Ed.), *Handbook of Research on Climate Change Impact on Health and Environmental Sustainability* (pp. 455–469). Hershey, PA: IGI Global. doi:10.4018/978-1-4666-8814-8.ch023

Minea, G., Bandoc, G., & Neculau, G. (2015). Seasonal Statistical Variability of Precipitations in Dobrogea and Danube Delta. In C. Maftei (Ed.), *Extreme Weather and Impacts of Climate Change on Water Resources in the Dobrogea Region* (pp. 1–16). Hershey, PA: IGI Global. doi:10.4018/978-1-4666-8438-6.ch001

Minhas, D. M., & Hussain, S. (2016). Efficient Control Strategies to Optimize Electricity Cost and Consumer Satisfaction. In A. Ahmad & N. Hassan (Eds.), *Smart Grid as a Solution for Renewable and Efficient Energy* (pp. 69–96). Hershey, PA: IGI Global. doi:10.4018/978-1-5225-0072-8.ch004

Mohapatra, M., & Baladhandautham, C. B. (2016). Implementation of Improved Control Strategy of DC-AC Converter using Delta-Sigma Modulator. In A. Ahmad & N. Hassan (Eds.), *Smart Grid as a Solution for Renewable and Efficient Energy* (pp. 249–272). Hershey, PA: IGI Global. doi:10.4018/978-1-5225-0072-8.ch011

Moustache, A. M. (2015). Adaptation to Impacts of Climate Change on the Food and Nutrition Security Status of a Small Island Developing State: The Case of the Republic of Seychelles. In W. Ganpat & W. Isaac (Eds.), *Impacts of Climate Change on Food Security in Small Island Developing States* (pp. 96–129). Hershey, PA: IGI Global. doi:10.4018/978-1-4666-6501-9.ch004

Mujere, N., & Moyce, W. (2017). Climate Change Impacts on Surface Water Quality. In W. Ganpat & W. Isaac (Eds.), *Environmental Sustainability and Climate Change Adaptation Strategies* (pp. 322–340). Hershey, PA: IGI Global. doi:10.4018/978-1-5225-1607-1.ch012

Mukherjee, S., & Chakraborty, D. (2016). Does Fiscal Policy Influence Per Capita CO2 Emission?: A Cross Country Empirical Analysis. In S. Dinda (Ed.), *Handbook of Research on Climate Change Impact on Health and Environmental Sustainability* (pp. 568–592). Hershey, PA: IGI Global. doi:10.4018/978-1-4666-8814-8.ch028

N'Yeurt, A. D., & Iese, V. (2015). Marine Plants as a Sustainable Source of Agri-Fertilizers for Small Island Developing States (SIDS). In W. Ganpat & W. Isaac (Eds.), *Impacts of Climate Change on Food Security in Small Island Developing States* (pp. 280–311). Hershey, PA: IGI Global. doi:10.4018/978-1-4666-6501-9.ch010

Nersesian, R. L., & Strang, K. D. (2017). Feasibility Approaches to Reduce the Unreliability of Gas, Nuclear, Coal, Solar and Wind Electricity Production. *International Journal of Risk and Contingency Management*, 6(1), 54–69. doi:10.4018/IJRCM.2017010104

Ngubevana, L. (2017). Sustainable Development Dilemmas of Biofuels Research and Production: A Snapshot in South Africa. *International Journal of Energy Optimization and Engineering*, 6(2), 24–41. doi:10.4018/IJEOE.2017040102

Nyangon, J., Alabbas, N., & Agbemabiese, L. (2017). Entangled Systems at the Energy-Water-Food Nexus: Challenges and Opportunities. In P. Rao & Y. Patil (Eds.), *Reconsidering the Impact of Climate Change on Global Water Supply, Use, and Management* (pp. 144–165). Hershey, PA: IGI Global. doi:10.4018/978-1-5225-1046-8.ch009

Onutai, S., Jiemsirilers, S., & Kobayashi, T. (2017). Geopolymer Sourced with Fly Ash and Industrial Aluminum Waste for Sustainable Materials. In T. Kobayashi (Ed.), *Applied Environmental Materials Science for Sustainability* (pp. 165–185). Hershey, PA: IGI Global. doi:10.4018/978-1-5225-1971-3.ch008

Osmani, A. R. (2016). Greenhouse Gas Mitigation through Energy Efficiency: Perform, Achieve, and Trade (PAT) – India's Emission Trading Scheme. In S. Dinda (Ed.), *Handbook of Research on Climate Change Impact on Health and Environmental Sustainability* (pp. 537–566). Hershey, PA: IGI Global. doi:10.4018/978-1-4666-8814-8.ch027

Osmani, A. R. (2017). Tipaimukh Multipurpose Hydroelectric Project: A Policy Perspective – Indo-Bangla Priorities, Indigenous Peoples' Rights, and Environmental Concerns. In P. Rao & Y. Patil (Eds.), *Reconsidering the Impact of Climate Change on Global Water Supply, Use, and Management* (pp. 227–251). Hershey, PA: IGI Global. doi:10.4018/978-1-5225-1046-8.ch013

Ozpinar, A., & Ozil, E. (2016). Smart Grid and Demand Side Management: Application of Metaheuristic and Artificial Intelligence Algorithms. In A. Ahmad & N. Hassan (Eds.), *Smart Grid as a Solution for Renewable and Efficient Energy* (pp. 49–68). Hershey, PA: IGI Global. doi:10.4018/978-1-5225-0072-8.ch003

Padigala, B. S. (2017). Traditional Water Management System for Climate Change Adaptation in Mountain Ecosystems. In P. Rao & Y. Patil (Eds.), *Reconsidering the Impact of Climate Change on Global Water Supply, Use, and Management* (pp. 9–32). Hershey, PA: IGI Global. doi:10.4018/978-1-5225-1046-8.ch002

Page, T. (2017). A Feasibility Study in Energy Harvesting from Piezoelectric Keyboards. *International Journal of Energy Optimization and Engineering*, *6*(2), 1–23. doi:10.4018/IJEOE.2017040101

Paul, S., & Roy, P. K. (2016). A Novel Optimization Algorithm for Transient Stability Constrained Optimal Power Flow. In P. Vasant & N. Voropai (Eds.), *Sustaining Power Resources through Energy Optimization and Engineering* (pp. 147–176). Hershey, PA: IGI Global. doi:10.4018/978-1-4666-9755-3.ch007

Pieroni, A., & Iazeolla, G. (2016). Engineering QoS and Energy Saving in the Delivery of ICT Services. In P. Vasant & N. Voropai (Eds.), *Sustaining Power Resources through Energy Optimization and Engineering* (pp. 208–226). Hershey, PA: IGI Global. doi:10.4018/978-1-4666-9755-3.ch009

Polprasert, J., Ongsakul, W., & Dieu, V. N. (2016). Improved Pseudo-Gradient Search Particle Swarm Optimization for Optimal Power Flow Problem. In P. Vasant & N. Voropai (Eds.), *Sustaining Power Resources through Energy Optimization and Engineering* (pp. 177–207). Hershey, PA: IGI Global. doi:10.4018/978-1-4666-9755-3.ch008

Potiyaraj, P. (2017). Poly (Lactic Acid) Generated for Advanced Materials. In T. Kobayashi (Ed.), *Applied Environmental Materials Science for Sustainability* (pp. 106–127). Hershey, PA: IGI Global. doi:10.4018/978-1-5225-1971-3.ch005

Rale, V., & Tendulkar, P. (2017). Common Duckweeds as a Model System for Climate Change Impact Assessment. In P. Rao & Y. Patil (Eds.), *Reconsidering the Impact of Climate Change on Global Water Supply, Use, and Management* (pp. 364–372). Hershey, PA: IGI Global. doi:10.4018/978-1-5225-1046-8.ch019

Ramakrishna, A., & Bang, S. (2015). The Impacts of Climate Change on Food Security and Management in Papua New Guinea. In W. Ganpat & W. Isaac (Eds.), *Impacts of Climate Change on Food Security in Small Island Developing States* (pp. 67–95). Hershey, PA: IGI Global. doi:10.4018/978-1-4666-6501-9.ch003

Rani, S. (2016). Assessment of Annual, Monthly, and Seasonal Trends in the Long Term Rainfall of the Garhwal Himalayas. In S. Dinda (Ed.), *Handbook of Research on Climate Change Impact on Health and Environmental Sustainability* (pp. 222–241). Hershey, PA: IGI Global. doi:10.4018/978-1-4666-8814-8.ch011

Rao, P., & Patil, Y. (2017). Recent Trends, Issues, and Challenges in Water Resource Development and Global Climate Change. In P. Rao & Y. Patil (Eds.), *Reconsidering the Impact of Climate Change on Global Water Supply, Use, and Management* (pp. 1–8). Hershey, PA: IGI Global. doi:10.4018/978-1-5225-1046-8.ch001

Ray, S. (2016). A Framework for Understanding Adaptation by Manufacturing Industries. In S. Dinda (Ed.), *Handbook of Research on Climate Change Impact on Health and Environmental Sustainability* (pp. 471–481). Hershey, PA: IGI Global. doi:10.4018/978-1-4666-8814-8.ch024

Roberts, T. G., & Rodriguez, M. T. (2015). An Overview of Climate Change and Impacts on Food Security in Small Island Developing States. In W. Ganpat & W. Isaac (Eds.), *Impacts of Climate Change on Food Security in Small Island Developing States* (pp. 1–31). Hershey, PA: IGI Global. doi:10.4018/978-1-4666-6501-9.ch001

Roşu, L., & Macarov, L. I. (2015). Management of Drought and Floods in the Dobrogea Region. In C. Maftei (Ed.), *Extreme Weather and Impacts of Climate Change on Water Resources in the Dobrogea Region* (pp. 403–443). Hershey, PA: IGI Global. doi:10.4018/978-1-4666-8438-6.ch013

Roşu, L., & Zăgan, R. (2015). Management of Drought and Floods in Romania. In C. Maftei (Ed.), *Extreme Weather and Impacts of Climate Change on Water Resources in the Dobrogea Region* (pp. 345–402). Hershey, PA: IGI Global. doi:10.4018/978-1-4666-8438-6.ch012

Roy, J., Ghosh, D., Mukhopadhyay, K., & Ghosh, A. (2016). Exacerbating Health Risks in India due to Climate Change: Rethinking Approach to Health Service Provision. In S. Dinda (Ed.), *Handbook of Research on Climate Change Impact on Health and Environmental Sustainability* (pp. 1–25). Hershey, PA: IGI Global. doi:10.4018/978-1-4666-8814-8.ch001

Roy, P. K. (2016). A Novel Evolutionary Optimization Technique for Solving Optimal Reactive Power Dispatch Problems. In P. Vasant & N. Voropai (Eds.), *Sustaining Power Resources through Energy Optimization and Engineering* (pp. 244–275). Hershey, PA: IGI Global. doi:10.4018/978-1-4666-9755-3.ch011

Roy, P. K., Dutta, S., & Nandi, D. (2016). Optimal Reactive Power Dispatch Incorporating TCSC-TCPS Devices Using Different Evolutionary Optimization Techniques. In P. Vasant & N. Voropai (Eds.), *Sustaining Power Resources through Energy Optimization and Engineering* (pp. 326–359). Hershey, PA: IGI Global. doi:10.4018/978-1-4666-9755-3.ch014

Roy, P. K., & Ghosh, M. (2017). Combined Heat and Power Dispatch using Hybrid Genetic Algorithm and Biogeography-based Optimization. *International Journal of Energy Optimization and Engineering*, 6(1), 49–65. doi:10.4018/IJEOE.2017010103

Samanta, D. (2016). Lack of Land Tenure Security as Challenges to Sustainable Development: An Assessment in the Context of Bihar, India. In S. Dinda (Ed.), *Handbook of Research on Climate Change Impact on Health and Environmental Sustainability* (pp. 348–362). Hershey, PA: IGI Global. doi:10.4018/978-1-4666-8814-8.ch017

Sasirekha, S., & Swamynathan, S. (2017). Fuzzy Rule Based Environment Monitoring System for Weather Controlled Laboratories using Arduino. *International Journal of Intelligent Information Technologies*, 13(1), 50–66. doi:10.4018/IJIIT.2017010103

Satoh, M. (2017). Metal Ion Separation with Functional Adsorbents and Phytoremediation Used as Sustainable Technologies. In T. Kobayashi (Ed.), *Applied Environmental Materials Science for Sustainability* (pp. 284–312). Hershey, PA: IGI Global. doi:10.4018/978-1-5225-1971-3.ch013

Scorza, F. (2016). Towards Self Energy-Management and Sustainable Citizens Engagement in Local Energy Efficiency Agenda. *International Journal of Agricultural and Environmental Information Systems*, 7(1), 44–53. doi:10.4018/IJAEIS.2016010103

Sen, S. K., & Pookayaporn, J. (2017). Role of Water-Energy-Waste Inter-Relatedness to Drive Sustainability amid Climate Concerns. In P. Rao & Y. Patil (Eds.), *Reconsidering the Impact of Climate Change on Global Water Supply, Use, and Management* (pp. 195–210). Hershey, PA: IGI Global. doi:10.4018/978-1-5225-1046-8.ch011

Senapati, S., & Gupta, V. (2016). Impacts of Climate Change on Fish Productivity: A Quantitative Measurement. In S. Dinda (Ed.), *Handbook of Research on Climate Change Impact on Health and Environmental Sustainability* (pp. 243–260). Hershey, PA: IGI Global. doi:10.4018/978-1-4666-8814-8.ch012

Senapati, S., & Gupta, V. (2016). Vulnerability to Climate Change: Issues and Challenges towards Developing Vulnerability Indicator. In S. Dinda (Ed.), *Handbook of Research on Climate Change Impact on Health and Environmental Sustainability* (pp. 82–104). Hershey, PA: IGI Global. doi:10.4018/978-1-4666-8814-8.ch005

Serban, C., & Maftei, C. (2015). Using Grid Computing and Satellite Remote Sensing in Evapotranspiration Estimation. In C. Maftei (Ed.), *Extreme Weather and Impacts of Climate Change on Water Resources in the Dobrogea Region* (pp. 145–173). Hershey, PA: IGI Global. doi:10.4018/978-1-4666-8438-6.ch006

Shanmuganathan, S., Narayanan, A., & Medagoda, N. P. (2016). Temporal Data Analysis and Mining Methods for Modelling the Climate Change Effects on Malaysia's Oil Palm Yield at Different Regional Scales. In S. Dinda (Ed.), *Handbook of Research on Climate Change Impact on Health and Environmental Sustainability* (pp. 482–513). Hershey, PA: IGI Global. doi:10.4018/978-1-4666-8814-8.ch025

Singh, R. K. (2017). Impact of Climate Change on the Retreat of Himalayan Glaciers and Its Impact on Major River Hydrology: Himalayan Glacier Hydrology. In P. Rao & Y. Patil (Eds.), *Reconsidering the Impact of Climate Change on Global Water Supply, Use, and Management* (pp. 70–83). Hershey, PA: IGI Global. doi:10.4018/978-1-5225-1046-8.ch005

Singh-Ackbarali, D., & Maharaj, R. (2017). Mini Livestock Ranching: Solution to Reducing the Carbon Footprint and Negative Environmental Impacts of Agriculture. In W. Ganpat & W. Isaac (Eds.), *Environmental Sustainability and Climate Change Adaptation Strategies* (pp. 188–212). Hershey, PA: IGI Global. doi:10.4018/978-1-5225-1607-1.ch007

Siwe, A. T., & Tembine, H. (2016). Energy Cost Saving Tips in Distributed Power Networks. In A. Ahmad & N. Hassan (Eds.), *Smart Grid as a Solution for Renewable and Efficient Energy* (pp. 26–48). Hershey, PA: IGI Global. doi:10.4018/978-1-5225-0072-8.ch002

Srivastava, N. (2016). Climate Change Mitigation: Collective Efforts and Responsibly. In S. Dinda (Ed.), *Handbook of Research on Climate Change Impact on Health and Environmental Sustainability* (pp. 427–439). Hershey, PA: IGI Global. doi:10.4018/978-1-4666-8814-8.ch021

Stennikov, V., Barakhtenko, E., Sokolov, D., & Oshchepkova, T. (2016). Problems of Modeling and Optimization of Heat Supply Systems: New Methods and Software for Optimization of Heat Supply System Parameters. In P. Vasant & N. Voropai (Eds.), *Sustaining Power Resources through Energy Optimization and Engineering* (pp. 76–101). Hershey, PA: IGI Global. doi:10.4018/978-1-4666-9755-3.ch004

Stennikov, V., Oshchepkova, T., & Stennikov, N. (2016). Problems of Modeling and Optimization of Heat Supply Systems: Methods to Comprehensively Solve the Problem of Heat Supply System Expansion and Reconstruction. In P. Vasant & N. Voropai (Eds.), *Sustaining Power Resources through Energy Optimization and Engineering* (pp. 26–53). Hershey, PA: IGI Global. doi:10.4018/978-1-4666-9755-3.ch002

Stennikov, V., Penkovskii, A., & Khamisov, O. (2016). Problems of Modeling and Optimization of Heat Supply Systems: Bi-Level Optimization of the Competitive Heat Energy Market. In P. Vasant & N. Voropai (Eds.), *Sustaining Power Resources through Energy Optimization and Engineering* (pp. 54–75). Hershey, PA: IGI Global. doi:10.4018/978-1-4666-9755-3.ch003

Stennikov, V. A., & Postnikov, I. V. (2016). Problems of Modeling and Optimization of Heat Supply Systems: Methodological Support for a Comprehensive Analysis of Fuel and Heat Supply Reliability. In P. Vasant & N. Voropai (Eds.), *Sustaining Power Resources through Energy Optimization and Engineering* (pp. 102–126). Hershey, PA: IGI Global. doi:10.4018/978-1-4666-9755-3.ch005

Stone, R. J. (2017). Modelling the Frequency of Tropical Cyclones in the Lower Caribbean Region. In W. Ganpat & W. Isaac (Eds.), *Environmental Sustainability and Climate Change Adaptation Strategies* (pp. 341–349). Hershey, PA: IGI Global. doi:10.4018/978-1-5225-1607-1.ch013

Swain, M. (2016). Vulnerability to Local Climate Change: Farmers' Perceptions on Trends in Western Odisha, India. In S. Dinda (Ed.), *Handbook of Research on Climate Change Impact on Health and Environmental Sustainability* (pp. 139–155). Hershey, PA: IGI Global. doi:10.4018/978-1-4666-8814-8.ch007

Swain, M., & Swain, M. (2016). Evolution and Efficacy of Drought Management Policies and Programmes: The Case of Western Odisha, India. In S. Dinda (Ed.), *Handbook of Research on Climate Change Impact on Health and Environmental Sustainability* (pp. 176–194). Hershey, PA: IGI Global. doi:10.4018/978-1-4666-8814-8.ch009

Takahashi, Y. (2017). Eco-Friendly On-Site Water Analyses for Ultra-Trace Harmful Ions. In T. Kobayashi (Ed.), *Applied Environmental Materials Science for Sustainability* (pp. 313–326). Hershey, PA: IGI Global. doi:10.4018/978-1-5225-1971-3.ch014

Taokaew, S., Phisalaphong, M., & Newby, B. Z. (2017). Bacterial Cellulose: Biosyntheses, Modifications, and Applications. In T. Kobayashi (Ed.), *Applied Environmental Materials Science for Sustainability* (pp. 255–283). Hershey, PA: IGI Global. doi:10.4018/978-1-5225-1971-3.ch012

Tauch, S., Liu, W., & Pears, R. (2016). Measuring Cascading Failures in Smart Grid Networks. In A. Ahmad & N. Hassan (Eds.), *Smart Grid as a Solution for Renewable and Efficient Energy* (pp. 208–225). Hershey, PA: IGI Global. doi:10.4018/978-1-5225-0072-8.ch009

Trang, T. T. (2017). Study on the Use of Biomass Polymer Sheets in Water/Alcohol Pervaporation as a Sustainable Source of Alcohol Energy. In T. Kobayashi (Ed.), *Applied Environmental Materials Science for Sustainability* (pp. 234–254). Hershey, PA: IGI Global. doi:10.4018/978-1-5225-1971-3.ch011

Tsiaras, S. (2017). Exploring the Impact of Tourism to the Sustainable Development of Mountain Regions: Implications of the Climatic Conditions. *International Journal of Agricultural and Environmental Information Systems*, 8(1), 14–28. doi:10.4018/IJAEIS.2017010102

Tugjamba, N., Yembuu, B., Gantumur, A., & Getsel, U. (2016). Policy Provisions and Teachers Needs on Climate Change Education for Sustainable Development in Mongolia. *International Journal of Asian Business and Information Management*, 7(4), 36–48. doi:10.4018/IJABIM.2016100103

Tyukhov, I., Rezk, H., & Vasant, P. (2016). Modern Optimization Algorithms and Applications in Solar Photovoltaic Engineering. In P. Vasant & N. Voropai (Eds.), *Sustaining Power Resources through Energy Optimization and Engineering* (pp. 390–445). Hershey, PA: IGI Global. doi:10.4018/978-1-4666-9755-3.ch016

Uddin, Z., Shah, N., Ahmad, A., Mehmood, W., & Alam, F. (2016). Signal Processing Techniques in Smart Grids. In A. Ahmad & N. Hassan (Eds.), *Smart Grid as a Solution for Renewable and Efficient Energy* (pp. 273–297). Hershey, PA: IGI Global. doi:10.4018/978-1-5225-0072-8.ch012

Ventrapragada, E. A., & Rayavarapu, N. (2017). Climate Change and Agriculture: Time for a Responsive and Responsible System of Water Management. In P. Rao & Y. Patil (Eds.), *Reconsidering the Impact of Climate Change on Global Water Supply, Use, and Management* (pp. 326–363). Hershey, PA: IGI Global. doi:10.4018/978-1-5225-1046-8.ch018

Wang, Q., & Liu, H. (2017). Optimized Base Station Sleeping and Renewable Energy Procurement Scheme Using PSO. *International Journal of Swarm Intelligence Research*, 8(1), 54–73. doi:10.4018/IJSIR.2017010103

Wong, J., & Lim, Y. S. (2016). Revolution of Energy Storage System in Smart Grids. In A. Ahmad & N. Hassan (Eds.), *Smart Grid as a Solution for Renewable and Efficient Energy* (pp. 181–206). Hershey, PA: IGI Global. doi:10.4018/978-1-5225-0072-8.ch008

Wu, Y., Tan, X., Qian, L. P., Tsang, D. H., Song, W., & Yu, L. (2016). Management of Scheduling and Trading in Hybrid Energy Trading Market. In A. Ahmad & N. Hassan (Eds.), *Smart Grid as a Solution for Renewable and Efficient Energy* (pp. 123–148). Hershey, PA: IGI Global. doi:10.4018/978-1-5225-0072-8.ch006

Xiang, M., Liu, W., Bai, Q., & Al-Anbuky, A. (2016). Dynamic Trust Elective Geo Routing to Secure Smart Grid Communication Networks. In A. Ahmad & N. Hassan (Eds.), *Smart Grid as a Solution for Renewable and Efficient Energy* (pp. 323–343). Hershey, PA: IGI Global. doi:10.4018/978-1-5225-0072-8.ch014

Zăgan, S., & Chiţu, M. (2015). The Influence of Air Temperature on the Quality Parameters of the Black Sea Coastal Waters. In C. Maftei (Ed.), *Extreme Weather and Impacts of Climate Change on Water Resources in the Dobrogea Region* (pp. 174–204). Hershey, PA: IGI Global. doi:10.4018/978-1-4666-8438-6.ch007

Zharkov, S. (2016). Assessment and Enhancement of the Energy Supply System Efficiency with Emphasis on the Cogeneration and Renewable as Main Directions for Fuel Saving. In P. Vasant & N. Voropai (Eds.), *Sustaining Power Resources through Energy Optimization and Engineering* (pp. 1–25). Hershey, PA: IGI Global. doi:10.4018/978-1-4666-9755-3.ch001

About the Author

Vangelis Marinakis is an Electrical and Computer Engineer of the National Technical University of Athens and holds a PhD in the research domain of decision support systems for sustainable local/regional energy planning. His experience and knowledge cover the fields of energy and environmental/climate policy, design and development of related multiple-criteria decision support systems, promotion of energy efficiency/renewable energy technologies and modern financing mechanisms, energy management in buildings (ISO 50001, etc.), design and development of innovative systems and Internet of Things (IoT) solutions for Smart Cities, elaboration of sustainable energy and climate action plans, and energy corporate responsibility of enterprises. Dr. Marinakis has participated as energy expert in European (Horizon 2020, FP7, IEE, etc.) and national projects, including among others OPTIMUS, ESCOCITY, eReNet, BETTER and EU-GCC CLEAN ENERGY NETWORK. He has more than 40 scientific publications in international journals and book chapters, as well as numerous announcements in national and international conferences.

Index